# 101 WAYS

## TO SUPERCHARGE
## YOUR PRODUCTIVITY

Marcham Publishing

© Dr. Monica Seeley and Melissa Esquibel 2021

All rights reserved.

Marcham Publishing

# 101 WAYS

## TO SUPERCHARGE
## YOUR PRODUCTIVITY

**Dr. Monica Seeley & Melissa Esquibel**

# TABLE OF CONTENTS

# FOREWORD

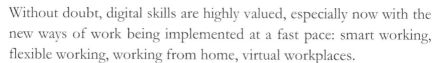

Without doubt, digital skills are highly valued, especially now with the new ways of work being implemented at a fast pace: smart working, flexible working, working from home, virtual workplaces.

This is an essential book, deeply significant in many ways, for both the tips, guidelines, and suggestions that it makes and the questions it raises about how we use the digital tools at our disposal.

Melissa Esquibel is known for her unique ability to make learning programs enjoyable and valuable, and for being a mainstay at administrative professional conferences. With Melissa, I have learned Excel tips that help me create and effectively manage event attendee lists. She made me become an Excel enthusiast.

Dr. Monica Seeley is a leading international expert on email best practice and has helped me handle my email inbox like a pro. This knowledge has also been used to create an Internal Corporate Communications Policy, which includes email management.

The authors' extensive experience training Assistants has enabled them to write a highly practical book. Each chapter (tip) presents a challenging situation and then proposes a solution, ready to be applied.

Why do Assistants need digital skills to get ahead in their careers? Digital skills enable one to work more effectively, pioneer the implementation of new tools, teach teammates to use these tools and be safe and legal online. This also means understanding best practice in data storage and sharing, and security and risk management against a cyberattack. This book will help you improve your digital literacy and ensure you have a seat in the future of work – where digital skills will be vital.

Being able to navigate a computer desktop (and mobile devices) quickly and efficiently has become more important than having a tidy desk. This book is for those of you who want to be not just adept with technology, but more agile and even the expert in your workplace. It enables this by presenting solutions that improve productivity, be they process or software driven.

Who does not want to have an assistant who improves processes and results? There is something for everyone at every level of digital expertise: from those already working in the digital sector itself to those wanting to advance their overall level of digital communications skills to be able to contribute more significantly in the age of digital business.

Julia Schmidt
Executive Assistant and author of
The Executive Support Guide to
Building a Successful Career Strategy

# DEDICATIONS

From Monica

For me, this book is an accumulation of the best tips and practices from 30+ years in the business of email management. It is dedicated to all the amazing PAs and EAs who have taught me so many of these nuggets over this time. Thank you all for enlightening my knowledge. A special debt of gratitude must also be paid to my own two EAs who have organised my life so well over the years, making sure I arrive at meetings on the right day and time, equipped with the correct files and digital device, namely Susan Oakes and Angela Peach. Thank you both.

Last but by no means least, this book would not have happened without the foresight of Lucy Brazier, who introduced me to Melissa Esquibel. After 30+ years, I thought I knew all there was to know about Microsoft Outlook until I started working with Melissa. Working together has been both a learning experience and great fun.

From Melissa

This book is dedicated to everyone that has ever been kind (and brave) enough to tell me when I was mistaken. This list is long and distinguished, and includes my brilliant co-author, Dr. Monica Seeley, my dear friend and mentor, Lucy Brazier, my amazing son and oracle, Zach Stout, my beautiful firebrand granddaughter, Lillian (who challenged my explanation of how our family is connected with 'That's not it, Grandma" when she was 4 years old) and my intrepid daughter-in-law, Jenny Gold, who is an expert at herding all of us cats.

I also dedicate this book to all the savvy administrative professionals I've met who have shared their tips, asked great questions and who fuel my passion for providing clarity in a cloudy world. You all rock. HARD!

Thank you all from the bottom of my heart. Ubuntu (I am because you are).

# INTRODUCTION

Have you ever wondered if there's a better, faster, more efficient, effective way to do something? Savvy administrative professionals ask this question each time they find themselves doing repetitive or unnecessarily complicated work. The authors' fondest hope is that this book puts an end to many of these challenges.

The book is organised according to the types of work that you do every day:

- Communicate with your colleagues (Effective Communication)
- Send email (Manageable Email)
- Manage tasks and teamwork (Teamwork and Tasks)
- Protect information (Cyber security)
- Manage calendars and diaries (Calendars and Diaries)
- Maintain your wellbeing (Looking After Yourself and the Planet)
- ...and all the rest! (that's actually what it's called!)

Each tip chapter begins with The Challenge. Some of these challenges came directly from you and people who do what you do. After this, you will find a section called The Solution. We have not attempted to divide this book by technology brand, because this will change for many of you. In fact, it might change as often as you inhale and exhale! It is also because many of you are working in environments where multiple technology platforms are in place. Exploring how the technology topics are broken down can help you uncover the same types of functionality in different technologies.

There are also many tips in this book that are related to keeping yourself (and the planet) well. There are ways in which all of us can lead in our teams and in our organisations that have to do with protecting our health and working in ways that reduce carbon-emissions. As administrative professionals, we are often the bellwether for the people with whom we work. They watch us and notice what we value. No matter where you stand on your own health or on environmental preservation, these tips will make you more productive and effective.

Whether you use this book as a reference book to help you solve everyday challenges, or as a source of inspiration as you randomly read a tip or two a week, we hope you find it something you pick up often and use to make your work life better.

# EFFECTIVE COMMUNICATION

# ‖ Tip #1 ‖

## Email, App or Text?

### The Challenge

In Tip 65, 'Consider Collaborative Tools', page 226, we explore popular apps that, among other things, facilitate communication. As the choices for means to communicate with colleagues expand, knowing which thing to use when can become confusing. The first step is to get consensus, followed by training and, finally, implementation.

### The Solution

Every organisation is different. Many will declare that all communications which are official should only use email. Others are more flexible, and still others don't use email at all internally. As mentioned in 'Consider Collaborative Tools', alternative, non-email methods of communication can generate their own email glut. Use of these for specific purposes should be accompanied by well-thought-out management of notifications and alerts. If you are only receiving instant alerts that indicate 'must read now', a more robust collection of communication mechanisms can be assembled into a strategic communication plan.

Here is a suggested way to identify what to use and by whom it should be used for various purposes.

| Purpose | By whom? | App |
|---|---|---|
| Meeting invitations/responses | Colleagues, Clients, Vendors | Email |
| Updates on projects | Colleagues | Collaboration apps |
| Quick questions, requests and associated replies | Colleagues | Text* or Collaboration Apps (with carefully managed alerts) |
| Urgent messages | Colleagues, Clients, Vendors | Text* |
| Formal documents requiring a business action | Clients, Vendors<br>Colleagues | Email<br>Collaboration apps** |
| Message to establish a legally supportable agreement | Colleagues, Clients, Vendors | Email |
| Message to record a personnel/HR request or action | Colleagues | Collaboration apps** or Email |

* If text messages (such as SMS from your smart phone) constitute communications that are business records, text logs should be managed by IT to ensure that an audit trail can be established.

** If a system with the proper access control and visibility is established in SharePoint or other internal intranet site, communications of this sort can be handled there. However, the mechanism to alert someone that a new item has been added or modified should be activated.

Be patient with colleagues, clients and vendors as they become accustomed to the best way to get a timely response to their questions and requests. Model best practices by responding to messages from anywhere in the appropriate channel.

# Tip #2

## Team Guidelines for Communication

Here we present tips for any office technology platform, including G Suite and Microsoft 365. In Tip 1, 'Email, App or Text', we discussed the various methods of communication and how they might be used. A company's culture and social fabric can dictate communication customs as well. However, when teams are working together to achieve a mutual goal, setting up ground rules for how you will communicate with one another can be a key success factor.

## The Challenge

Without a well-understood framework for communication, time is wasted;, messages are left unread or lost in the sea of other email, text and other messages. The domino effect is too much 'nag mail', missed deadlines and frustrated team members.

## The Solution

### What

When the team objective is established, the next step is the framework in which you will accomplish it. First, decide what types of communication can be expected.

- Status reports
- Physical location
- Alerts ("I'm running late for a meeting, be there in 5 minutes.")
- Formal communications between the team and others, intracompany
- Formal communications between the team and others, externally
- Help/information requests, urgent and otherwise
- Meetings/collaborations

## Where

If the members of your team can go to one place or platform to communicate, share information and collaborate, your communication strategy will have a better chance of success. For example, if you can skip email altogether when communicating amongst yourselves or internally with other members of your organisation, important messages will not get lost in the email haystack. Apps like Teams or tools like Groups in G Suite, and other platforms and apps such as SharePoint, OneNote, Monday.com, Slack and Trello, suit this purpose well.

If your project team is small, a single group or channel will suffice. If it is more complex, you may want to utilise a shallow, but meaningful, hierarchical arrangement such as channels in Teams or sub folders in file storage platforms. However, consider it carefully. Hierarchical structures seem organised, but often result in confusion about where things go and who can see them. In general, establish a hierarchy if access requirements make it necessary or confusion will be allayed rather than exacerbated.

## How and When

Setting expectations for how and when team members will be updated about things that affect their role in the project can feed everyone's productivity. Now that you've decided where communication, collaboration and information sharing will take place, it's time to preempt over- and under-communication. No team member should feel obligated to send 'nag mail' for information they require to complete their tasks, except if such a request is outside the scope of the established task plan. Likewise, all team members should know where to look for current status information and to locate deliverables that are complete or in the works. It should become the custom on a team for members to be self-sufficient in locating what they need. When this is easy, compliance is supported. When it is complicated, it will almost certainly result in over-communication. The expectation of self-sufficiency is something that should be established at the beginning of a project or when the team is first assembled.

Establish templates and locations for communicating status on a regular basis. Decide what all team members need to know and how frequently they should be updated. For example, if team members have tasks which depend upon the completion of tasks assigned to other team members, a 'mini' status message can be compiled like the following:

- *Task #[n] is complete. The deliverable is located in [linked document]. It was originally due on [date] and actually completed [on time or late/ early completion date].*

- *Task #[n] was due to be completed on [date] but has been delayed by [ reason]. I expect to complete it on [date ].*

---

**Pro Tip:**

If you are using Outlook email to communicate, this text can be created as a Quick Part. If it is normally communicated with a cc: to the project coordinator or sponsor, a Quick Step might be easier. Quick Parts are also a feature of Microsoft Word, making it easy to pre-assemble a message in Word and copy/paste it to whatever platform is being used to convey it.

---

Otherwise, weekly or monthly status reports can include a summary of tasks completed (see the box tip below if you are using OneNote), a statement about whether the project is on time, late or ahead of schedule, and any scope changes. If you have utilised features of your app or platform which make it apparent what has been completed, then include a simple message that it is time to review the project status and respond with any notes on new, late or removed tasks. Most platforms you might use for this purpose have a messaging component or a single email address which can be used. See the tip above about using Quick Parts for this purpose.

---

**Pro Tip:**

If you are using OneNote desktop and custom 'To Do" tags for each team member, use the Tag Summary to generate a quick status report. It will list tasks by team member and whether they're complete or not. Establish a standard of linking or placing the deliverable in the notebook itself and using the copy link to page or paragraph feature to easily navigate from task line item to deliverable.

---

## Bottom Line

Poor communication, whether too much, not enough, overly detailed or missing information:

- wastes time,
- causes rework,
- results in missed target dates,
- and, ultimately chips away at good working relationships.

# Tip #3

## Communicating via Social Media

## The Challenge

In the old days, if you wanted to communicate something you had very few choices: pick up the phone, send a letter or walk over to someone's desk. These days, you can communicate by so many methods, each of which seem to be at your fingertips and at the ready to communicate the next thought that pops into your head. This is both good and bad. Often because we can do this we don't take the time to think about whether that next thought should actually see the light of day and, if it should, if it is being transmitted across a communications channel that can afford it the proper level of security and safety. Even a moment's thought to the questions below can save an organisation from:

- data loss due to improper storage and archive;
- data theft due to unsecure channels;
- unauthorised access resulting in improper disclosure.

## The Solution

If your organisation's culture is informal and the preferred method of communicating everyday news and updates is something other than email, consider using social platforms like Yammer, Teams, or add-ons for G Suite like Happeo or Forum.

Publicly available apps like Facebook, LinkedIn or Hangouts may not afford the proper level of protection against data loss or unauthorised access.

Establish policies about what can be shared on internal and external social platforms. An effective social media policy should address:

- What can be shared on 'all employee' internal social platforms.
- What can be shared on public social platforms.
- Who to contact when in doubt.
- Actions to take when you see inappropriate communications.

Many employees believe that by using a pseudonym on social media (a no-no in many platforms' usage policies), making the subjects of their posts anonymous, and communicating only in 'closed groups', they are protecting themselves and their co-workers. Often, however, the breadcrumb trails are very easy to follow for anyone wanting to discover more than what has been provided. Responsible use of social media for employees needs to be well-understood. Include examples of inappropriate and appropriate posts on internal and external social channels.

Burying such information inside an organisation's formal communication policy may result in it being quickly forgotten. If it must be included, regular reminders, pop-up information screens and mentions in meetings can all work towards keeping the guardrails intact on the company information highway.

For guidance on social media policies, visit the SHRM (Society for Human Resources Management) and ACFE (Association of Certified Fraud Examiners) websites. You will also find a wealth of sample policies in a search for 'social media policies for employees'. Always obtain legal advice and guidance when establishing these policies to make sure that they follow local and national government regulations, as well as professional and industry association ethics.

# | Tip #4 |

## Communication Style: Yours or Theirs?

If you want to blow up social media, start a conversation on formal vs. informal communication styles, the use of contractions, (like it's and won't), or including emojis in an email. And don't even get us started on one space vs. two spaces after the full stop or the Oxford comma! Another debated topic is the use of titles like Mr, Ms, Sir, Madam, or their plurals, Messrs, Sirs and Mesdames. At no other time in the history of the worldwide workforce have there been so many generations in the office. Some of these choices will tend to be across those generational lines. Others depend on where people received their education and training. If blowing up social media isn't your prime objective, then the topic needs discussion before you can make the appropriate choices.

## The Challenge

How you decide communication style, punctuation usage and salutations can determine how well you are heard. When you've never communicated with someone, it becomes a real quandary for some. Why only for some? Because many forge ahead with the training they've received without regard for the acceptance of their messages, believing firmly that they are right and everyone else will simply know it or feel ashamed of their rudeness. OK, that may be going a bit far. Suffice it to say there is room for flexibility. So, where to start?

## The Solution

Before deciding on how best to put your message forward, determine what you want to have happen as a result of your communication.

- Do you want them to buy something?
- Would you like their cooperation on a project?
- Are you offering them employment?
- Do you want to correct their misstep?
- Would you like them to forgive you for one of your own missteps?

In each of these cases, there is an objective that involves the other party agreeing to something you are communicating. Think like a marketing or advertising person. What style of communication will work best? You might think, for example, that trying to sound 'hip' and informal will help you gain cooperation from one of your younger co-workers. Perhaps it will, but see if you would be comfortable saying those words out loud to them in the hall or on the phone. If not, maybe your own style of informal would be good enough. You may hear them greet each other with 'Yo!' or as 'dude,' but don't do so yourself if it would feel uncomfortable. On the other hand, if this is their method of communication, perhaps rethink a 'Dear Sir' or beginning a paragraph with 'In regards to your earlier communication…'

The bottom line is: take some time to learn about those with whom you need to communicate, and think through what you would like to have them willingly do because they feel comfortable that communicating with you is worth the effort. Be willing to shift your communication style to better fit your organisation, colleagues or customers. Being right isn't as much fun as getting things done.

**Pro Tip:**

Apps like Grammarly offer proofreading for communication style, for example, academic vs. business. If you're having trouble making a needed shift, a Grammarly subscription may be ideal.

# Tip #5

## The Polite Chaser Email

## The Challenge

How do you send a polite reminder email to someone asking for a reply to your email? Before we look at solutions, it might interest you to know that below are the most annoying phrases in an email.

| Annoying Phrase | Most hated by |
|---|---|
| Not sure if you saw my last email... | 25% |
| Per my last email... | 13% |
| Per our conversation... | 11% |
| Any updates on this? | 11% |
| Sorry for the double email. | 10% |
| Please advise. | 9% |
| As previously stated... | 9% |
| As discussed... | 6% |
| Re-attaching for convenience. | 6% |

This was based on research carried out by Adobe in 2018. So, what does this leave us?

## The Solution

No one likes to chase people for a response, and especially if the other person is very senior. Here is a four-point template to follow.

1. Keep the follow-up short.
2. Assume the recipient is busy and might just have missed your original email.
3. Remind them about the content and, if appropriate, the urgency of their response.
4. Re-attach any relevant files.

Use this template here for what a typical reminder email might say.

---

Hi Jack,

I know you're busy as we approach year end. We've agreed the training budget for next year and now shortlisted potential providers. I'd really like to secure The ABC Training Co as they have very good reviews.

Do you have time this week to review the short-list and give me your opinion? Would it help if we scheduled a conference call; looks like you have some free time on Thursday.

---

If this approach fails, you can always try inserting a reminder flag in the next email. Maybe even have the subject-line turn red when it enters their inbox! See Tip 62, 'Insert a Reminder in a Recipient's Email', page 217.

# | Tip #6 |

## Punctuation Is Important

## The Challenge

We are all time poor and busy. We are used to text-speak on social media apps, where either there is auto text or it doesn't matter if we make a typo, miss a comma, forget a full stop and so on. The question we are often asked in this digital age is, 'Do I really need to bother using correct punctuation with email?'

The answer is 'yes,' for five main reasons.

1. It makes it easier for the recipient to read and hence respond properly to your message.
2. Proper punctuation reduces the scope for a misunderstanding, which at worst can result in an email war, another email-gate disaster or HR tribunal. All of these are expensive, not least because they can damage your reputation.
3. Correct punctuation makes it easy for the recipient to read your message and reduces the potential rounds of email ping-pong, which saves everyone's time and helps improve performance.
4. The email you send is your digital dress code. The recipient may never have physically met you, (for example, if they are a customer, in another department, or an external supplier). Sloppy email implies sloppy you.

5. Email can be used as evidence. You would not want to leave anything you wrote open to interpretation.

Consider the example below.

- Richard is going to be the new Marketing Director.
- Richard is going to be the new Marketing Director?
- Richard is going to be the new Marketing Director!

These each have different meanings based on the way they are punctuated. The first is a statement of fact. The second is a question:, is this true or gossip? The exclamation mark on the third implies emotions such as amazement (is he capable?), excitement (best man for the job) or perhaps anger at his appointment.

Look at these sentences again and ask yourself, what are you trying to say? How might the recipient judge you? The question mark could be anger because you did not get the job, or frustration because you think he is not capable and someone else you know is. The exclamation mark could be, genuine excitement because Richard is so good, or excitement because you are having a secret affair with Richard.

## The Solution

We were all taught punctuation at school, but it's easy to forget some of the basic lessons which help everyone be more productive. The key is to keep your sentences short and neutral (not emotional).

There are seven top forms of punctuation which help you create a professional image, save time and reduce the scope for any misunderstanding.

1. *Full stop* – Used to separate complete ideas which, if written as one sentence using a comma, would not make sense.
2. *Comma* – Used to separate items in a list, but remember you don't need a comma before the 'and' at the end of the list. Alternatively, it is used for joining separate short phrases which are linked.

For example:

Anne thought she brought a latte coffee, but when she opened it realised it was a cappuccino.

3. *Apostrophe (inverted comma)* – Used to show that either an item belongs to someone or that a letter in the word is missing. Examples of correct uses are:

   - Don't fill the printer paper tray to full otherwise it will jam.
   - The director's case is on the table. One director's case is on the table. The directors' cases are on the table. The cases of many directors are on the table.

Its versus It's. 'Its' without the apostrophe means that something in the sentence belongs to someone or something. Take this sentence: 'The webinar will be run by Jane. Its focus is on time management.' Here, 'its' refers to the webinar. 'It's' with an apostrophe means that two words have been joined together – 'it' and 'is' or 'has'. The golden rule for deciding which one to use is, if you insert the word 'is' or 'has' after 'it', 'does the sentence make sense?' If you took the second sentence above and wrote 'It is focus' it would not make sense. But 'it's not being run today' would make sense, ie 'it is not being run today'.

4. *Colon* – For linking two ideas together. Take these two examples.

   - Lucy went for a ride. There was a band playing in the park.
   - Lucy went for a ride: there was a band playing in the park.

The first sentence suggests that the two facts are not connected. The second implies Lucy went for a ride to the park to hear the band.

5. *Semi-colon* - This is used to connect two related ideas which might otherwise make a very short complete sentence, and hence to avoid the use of words such as 'and', 'yet', 'but' and 'while'.

For example: 'I opened a good bottle of wine today; life is too short to drink bad wine."

It can be hard to decide when to use a semi-colon and when to use a colon. A rule of thumb is, to use a colon to separate specific items related to a general statement. For example:

- I like most red fruits: plums and raspberries are my favourites.

A semi-colon connects two complete sentences without using the words 'and', 'yet', 'while' or 'but':

- I like most red fruits; it's easier to make jam from plums and raspberries.

6. *Quotation marks* - First, let's take the obvious use which is to indicate either unusual words or what a person said, as shown in the examples below.
   - The 'chardonnay' grape is very versatile and can be used to make a range of wine, from very dry like 'Pouilly Fuissé' to complex and rich like 'Meursault'.
   - Chelsea said 'The insurance premium will be the same as last year.'

Second, is it double or single quotation marks? Which you use is to some extent a matter of choice, although British English tends towards single quotes while in American English it's usually double quotes. The golden rule is: don't mix them in a single piece of content.

The only time to mix the two is to indicate a special word within a quotation. Use the alternative to that used for the main quotation as shown below.

- David said that if we travel to Burgundy 'we can taste some very good examples of the different styles of wine made from the 'chardonnay' grape.'

7. Parentheses - These are used to add extra meaning to the information before the parentheseis. They are not essential but may help the recipient understand what you are saying.
   - Jane (last year's EA of the Year) is expected to be a judge on this year's panel.

In this example, the phrase in parentheses is not essential; it tells someone who might not know Jane more about her credentials and why she is being asked to be a judge. For more on the subject, the best book is still 'Eats Shoots & Leaves' by Lynne Truss.

# ‖ Tip #7 ‖

## Walk and Talk Rather Than Email

*7% of a message was derived from the words, 38% from the intonation,*
*and 55% from the facial expression or body language.*
*— Albert Mehrabian*

## The Challenge

Technology makes it so easy to opt out of delivering a difficult message and avoid seeing the recipient's reactions. How often do you receive an email from a colleague and think to yourself, 'Why did they not talk to me?' Typical common examples are:

- The sender is sitting within a five-desk radius of you.
- It's very urgent.
- It's bad news.
- The email is very long and complex, leaving you trying to work out what the real issue is.

We are writing this book during the Covid-19 pandemic, and you might be thinking that walking and talking is not an option. No doubt the new normal office life will be different from before the pandemic, but some people will still work in an office. In fact, some never left the office. Regardless of the situation, we need to stop and think whether or not the most effective way to communicate is via a conversation either in person or via video conference.

The two challenges here are, how to:

- Recognise when to talk rather than send an email.
- Convince others to do the same.

Both are even harder if either you or the sender is more of an introvert than an extrovert. Introverts are renowned for hiding and managing by email. Furthermore, you might argue that it takes longer to talk and, in our time-poor world, this is just another burden.

## The Solution

### *Overall guidelines*
Good communications are about quality and not the speed with which they are delivered. Furthermore, there is some evidence to suggest that the greater the distance between the message deliverer and the recipient, the greater the scope to lie.

It is important to establish some guidelines for both yourself and those with whom you work most.

Here are seven overall guidelines for when a conversation is generally better than an email. Conversation implies, in priority order, face-to-face (real or video conference) followed by the phone.

- *Urgent and high priority* – the content needs a very rapid response. Never assume the other person is reading their email as it arrives.

- *Three to five rounds of email have been exchanged* – still there is no progress.

- *Five-desk radius* – and especially if the subject is ephemeral, or in other words does not form a necessary business record.

- *Complex content* – many different aspects to what needs to be communicated. It would be more effective to establish the whole picture synchronously rather than trying to piece it together through email messages, which are asynchronous. Yes, one of you will probably need to write a summary of the discussion but this is still better than playing constant email ping-pong during which either key points will be missed, or a misunderstanding can easily happen, especially if there are language barriers.

- *Bad news* – which may well unbalance the recipient, meaning that you need to see their reaction to help them through the situation. As a point of principle, you should never fire someone remotely, although there have been cases where this has happened.

- *Reprimanding a person for bad behaviuor or performance* – before doing so it is crucial to talk first to gain an insight into what their personal circumstances are. Maybe they are under immense personal stress from home, perhaps dealing with an elderly parent, sick child, etc. In troubled times and in a highly competitive job market, it is easy to cover up one's personal problems for fear of losing one's position.

- *You feel angry/emotional* – never, ever send an email. Write it and leave it in the draft box. If after a few hours you are still simmering and feeling upset, first, if it's not obvious, try to identify rationally what has caused your emotional reaction. Second, decide if the cause is genuine. Then make the effort to talk to the sender. Easy to say, hard to do, but you might find you come out on top, either having seen things from a different perspective or at the very least stopped a potentially harmful email war.

## *Other scenarios*

In addition to these seven golden rules, there are some other scenarios when a conversation might be far more effective than an email.

1. *Raising your profile / growing your network.* Maybe you met someone at an event and you want to impress them. Clearly, a starting point is to send them some information they might find helpful. Then follow this up with a phone call or walk and talk if you both are in the same office. Email can easily be overlooked but a conversation cannot, which allows you to convey your professional image in full.

2. *Negotiations.* Again, email is an obvious starting point but so often getting to 'yes' is much more quickly done by walking and talking. Do you ever see a car salesperson or estate agent clinch a sale by email? Not very often. Even in this digital world, nothing beats a conversation to negotiate your way to 'yes' by closing off all the potential objections as they come out during the negotiation.

3. *Asking a favour.* This is much the same as above. You can use your facial expressions and body language to help your case.

4. *Saying no / cancelling.* The converse of asking a favour. Maybe you are truly overstretched yet do not want to dent your relationship with the person asking for help. Walking and talking and using body and facial language helps soften the blow yet keep the business relationship intact. You may even detect from their body language that you may have to re-prioritise to support them and avert a possible disaster. None of this would be apparent through an email exchange.

5. *Language barriers.* The other person's mother tongue is not yours and your mastery of their language may not be that good. There are two sides to this situation. Some would argue that translation software mitigates this challenge, but it does not always translate the text properly, especially if the words are complex, unusual, jargon or colloquialisms. Furthermore, translation software does not show you both if you have understood each other properly. The general rule in this situation is: the more complex the content and the more likely it is for questions to surface, the more you should opt to speak face-to-face.

## Hidden benefits of walking and talking over email

Email is a very lean communications channel, just one step better than SMS and messaging apps like WhatsApp. Talking face-to-face is the richest way to communicate because you can see the other person's reaction instantly.

Besides the benefits outlined, there are some other pluses to walking and talking. These include:

1. *Improving wellbeing.* As we discuss in Tips 85, 86 and 87, it's important to move around and not sit all day in front of a digital device.

2. *Saving time.* Research indicates that one conversation can be up to 34 times more effective than any number of email messages, especially when trying to persuade someone to do something, (for instance complete a survey, take on a new task, give money, etc).

3. *Learning more and seeing the wider picture.* Email provides a blinkered view of the world. You might be working on Project/Client A, and as you walk through (or connect by conference call), you pick up information about Project/Client B, which feeds usefully into your project. One of our clients installed several whiteboards strategically placed across a large office. The original idea was to reduce the volume of trivial email messages (e.g., cakes to celebrate a birthday). However, everyone

commented that they loved to go and look at other group's whiteboards to see what else was happening in other teams for the cross-pollination of ideas, job opportunities etc.

4. *Raising your profile and network.* An email can easily be overlooked. But a person standing in front of your desk? Use the walk and talk option to create an impression on key people you want to impress.

5. *Realigning a conversation to gain a positive outcome.* As you see the person's reaction, you can immediately change the direction of the conversation to try to obtain a positive outcome even if the conversation is to convey bad news. You can at least make sure you do not leave the other person feeling as resentful as they might through an email; you can pick up on non-verbal cues and find something positive to say as they move forward.

6. *Contributing to reducing carbon emissions* – See Tips 93 and 94.

7. Creating a role model and leadership for communicating more effectively.

## *Moving forward*

Some business professionals avoid both the phone and email altogether if possible, opting instead for text messaging and communicating through social media or collaboration apps. Picking up the phone for many of these people is an absolute last resort. So, what hope do you have of engaging your 'talk resistant' colleagues, to actually converse when appropriate? Remember that your behaviour and attitude will affect how others behave, as shown below (in what is otherwise known as Betari's Box). As you (and, where relevant, your boss) make small but significant changes, others will accept that this is acceptable for them.

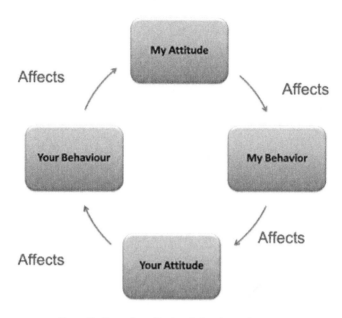

*Betari's Box for effecting behaviour change*

In the background, you can initiate some fun activities. For example, as one client did, place a tin of goodies on your desk to entice people to come and talk to you rather than firing off an email. In the Covid-19 era and beyond, when people are working more often from home, you might make that a donation to your (or the organisation's) favourite charity.

# Tip #8

# Live Videoconferencing Dos and Don'ts

Organizations are having more and more meetings with remote participants. Whether you're using Zoom, Team, GoToMeeting or another portal, most have the capability to have live video feed from your computer's camera. So-called 'Brady Bunch' views can show each participant's video feed in a tile, so that everyone can see everyone else.

## The Challenge

It can be a little disconcerting the first time you recognise that your brain thinks you're on a regular conference call, but your camera misses NOTHING!

## The Solution

Here are 10 top tips to keep you and your colleagues on task and not distracted by what's going on in everyone's video tile. They will also help make the conference call a more productive use of everyone's time.

1. Unless you need your phone to participate in the meeting, keep it out of sight. Otherwise you will be tempted to keep looking

down at it to see if anyone has liked your most recent social media post or sent you a new chat message.

2. To the extent possible, keep pets, children, and anything that is voice-activated out of your working space. That said, if by keeping your dog out of your workspace you've created another type of distraction (-endless barking), maybe try to keep Fido content at your feet.

3. Dress how you wish to be seen, head to toe. I know, you're thinking, 'But they can't see my pyjama bottoms!' That is true, until you have to get up out of your chair for a moment to deal with a spilled cup of coffee or the barking dog.

4. With many apps, you can blur the background or create a 'fake' background to show on your tile. Make sure whatever background you choose isn't also distracting in another way. If you're going to use a background different than your own real one, try to keep your background as plain as possible and do not wear the same colour as the background. Otherwise you could become just a floating head on the screen. I can't imagine anything more distracting than that!

5. Keep your own mic on mute until it's your turn to speak. Encourage others to do the same. The bigger the meeting, the more potential for background audio distractions.

6. Use the chat box to paste links to documents needed for the meeting or links to sites you are referencing.

7. Keep in mind that while you are looking at something else on your screen, your camera is still picking up where your eyes are moving. This might not be a problem, but don't get caught making faces you don't want everyone to see.

8. Before you get up from your chair, if possible, click off your video feed. Most apps will display your name or initials, indicating that you are still connected, but your camera is off.

9.  Whenever possible, if you are the meeting leader, assign someone else to monitor the chat to make sure that help is available for those having problems connecting to the audio or video, or for those who have questions on how to participate.

10. If you are recording the meeting, once everyone arrives, tell them. In many locations, it is illegal to record a conversation without consent from all parties. With our teams becoming further and further apart, there's no way to determine which locations have the rule and which don't. Best to be on the safe side. Also, about midway through the meeting, remind people that the session is being recorded. If possible, give people an opportunity to participate without video or to be a passive listener if they are not comfortable with the recording process.

# Tip #9

## Crystal Clear Subject Lines

### The Challenge

The subject line is the most important part of the email next to your name. It's what catches the recipient's eye and, in many cases, informs their decision about dealing with your email.

You receive at least 50 email messages a day and often triage them by either the sender or subject line. What if the subject line is not clear: maybe it's the same as the one from a previous email but contains new information about a new topic? Worse still, what if there is nothing in the subjectline?

Chances are, you will move on to the next email, and the first one might go unanswered for longer than it should. This could be expensive-, a missed request for information from a colleague for a client, late submission of a report which means someone else has to work late to sort out a problem, etc.

Whose fault is it if the email is not given the right attention and answered on time? The sender's.

## The Solution

Make the subject line crystal clear about not only the content of your email messages but also the date by which you need action (if at all). Here are five tips on how to use the subject line to help recipients to respond to your email messages (or not, as appropriate).

1. Tell them by when you need action as shown below.

   - The final agenda for the Monday 25 June Conference Call – Action by 20 June.

2. Never start writing about a new topic using an old subject line which is related to a previous discussion. Start a new email when you change topics.

3. When you receive an email with no subject line, insert one when replying.

4. When writing about the same topic and the thread is becoming long, either start a new email or edit the subject line to reflect the direction of change of the conversation as shown below.

   - Email messages 1-3: The revised sales training for next year
   - Email 4: The revised sales training for next year – Shortlist of providers
   - Email 5: The revised sales training for next year – Chosen provider

5. Use common abbreviations at the end of the subject line to indicate what action should be taken. Here are some common ones which help save everyone time and unnecessary rounds of email ping-pong.

   a) NRN – no reply necessary. The email contains a statement of fact and there is no need to acknowledge receipt of it, how you feel about it, etc. For example: 'The appointment of the new CEO will be announced on March 20 at 15.30 – NRN'.

b) FYI – for your information. Only reply if you see a potential problem;, otherwise assume I've taken action.

c) EOM – end of message. I've said all there is to say in the subject line. For example: 'Running 10 minutes late – EOM'.

d) WFM – working from home. It tells the other person you are neither in the office nor on a customer site. It might also imply that there could be a delay as your broadband is slow, or you are looking after someone but still working. It's become more popular since Covid-19.

e) LET – leaving early today. It sets expectations that if the recipient wants a reply to their reply, they had better send it earlier rather than later in the day.

# | Tip #10 |

## Don't Bury the Lead! Writing a Good Email

## The Challenge

Are people not responding to your email messages? One of the reasons may be that they are not clear about what you want them to do. As text messaging has taken over the short communication, email has become the actual business document. As such, it deserves a proper review and edit to make sure that it doesn't become a rambling, multi-paragraph puzzle for the recipient to solve. Email messages that are 'streams of consciousness' are often misunderstood or not even read to the end.

## The Solution

Don't bury the lead!
Consider keywords in subject lines that make it clear what the recipient might need to do. (See the previous Tip, 'Crystal Clear Subject Lines'.) If there is a date by which they must respond, include that, too!

## KISS

Keep It Short and Sweet. While what you initially write may come straight from your brain and onto the page, edit it to make sure you've said only what needs to be said, with the most important information first. Also, avoid creative fonts, emoticons/emojis or other embellishments to try to indicate tone. That said, if a diagram or graphic will help communicate your message, use the simplest forms.

## Just the Facts

Especially with messages in which you are requesting a response or an action, bullet point or number those things which are required, and label them with who should take the action in the case of multiple recipients. Only if absolutely necessary for clarity's sake should you provide a rationale or justification for your request. Otherwise, leave this part out. If the request is a sensitive one, it might be worth a preliminary phone call or chat, so that when the message is received, only the essential information is included.

## Test

Read only the first three sentences of the email message. Does it encourage the recipient to read further or draw the reader to the close button? As funny as it sounds, your email message is not about you, it's about the recipient.

# | Tip #11 |

## Email Etiquette: Text vs. Emoticons

## The Challenge

Is it OK to use emoticons or emojis in a business email?

## The Solution

The instinctive reaction is to say no, because a business email is a formal business record. As such, they can be produced as evidence in court and are open to misinterpretation. For example, what level of relationship does a smiley represent in an email between two people who are not close colleagues? Even when used only in internal email, you may have no control over whether the recipient will forward your message to someone else.

Let's take a more detailed look at the advantages and disadvantages of emoticons and emojis in business email.

### Advantages

- They can act as a substitute for the warm feeling conveyed, such as a smile or handshake when you meet a person face-to-face

- They can help build relationships in the absence of the personal touch. Those that have been accustomed to communicating this way on their journey to a professional career may prefer it.
- Emoticons and emojis can create a feeling of approachability, honesty and openness which might be hard to convey in words.
- They can serve as a quick way to respond to an email if you are very pressed for time.
- Used in the subject-line there is some evidence to suggest they increase the open rate, especially when used for direct marketing.

## Disadvantages

- Some people prefer to maintain a formal business relationship, and the use of an emoticon or emoji can be perceived as changing the level of formality.
- They can easily be misinterpreted and misunderstood. What is a joke to one person might be irritating or even offensive to another.
- There is some research evidence to suggest that the recipient may perceive you as less competent because you did not write a proper response.
- They are not universally understood across generational or geographical lines.

## In Summary

Know your recipient and use this abbreviated way of communicating only if you feel it is the right level of working relationship. Mirroring is a good guideline: if a sender uses them with you, then you can assume it is OK to use them with that person. However, be aware of the caveat at the beginning of this Tip; that an email is a formal business record, internally or externally.

If you can't decide, it is probably a wise choice to avoid using emojis with those senior to you in the organisation (regardless of whether they use them), when the email contains bad news or if there is the slightest chance of ambiguity. The last two instances are the time to choose your words carefully so that they convey the right message the first time.

# Tip #12

## Signature Line Etiquette

## The Challenge

Over the past few months, several EAs have asked us what makes a good signature on an email message. The question has reared its head again because they tell us that not only are signature blocks growing ever longer, but some people now include preferred pronouns. Our EAs and PAs often ask us, too, what do preferred pronouns mean and why use them?

## The Solution

The answer is almost two sides of the same coin. On the one hand, this is part of your digital dress and as such a great place to promote yourself and your organisation. On the other hand, think of the recipient who is reading your message on a mobile device, especially a phone. The signature block might take up more space than the actual content.

In many cases you may have no choice over the content of the signature which is automatically attached to your message: someone in your organisation will have specified it. Nonetheless, you might be able to add some important extra data just under your name.

Choice or no-choice, the golden rule is to keep your signature as short as possible and preferably no more than five lines long. Below are eight of the key items you should make sure you include if relevant.

## Top Eight Items to Include in Your Signature

1. Contact phone number. Yes, this is still the number one item to include in international format, for example +44 (0)12345 6789. Be warned, it is better to omit the local first digit (and brackets) because you cannot tap the number and dial from it. For the number here, ideally it should be +441234 56789.

2. Job title. Tell people who you are and, as appropriate, to whom you are the PA/EA.

3. *Website.* Particularly for those who are virtual PAs and EAs.

4. Social media icons. Your internet / social media profile is very important: pick at most three channels which portray you in the best light and of which you are most proud. No more than three, because it otherwise starts to look as though you are lacking focus and all over the place. Use icons if you can because they are universally recongised.

5. How to book a meeting with you. This is common practice amongst journalists and PR people and makes it easy to find you and book a meeting. Internally you might be able to share a link directly to your calendar. Externally this might be harder; simply state your preferred method. For example, to book a meeting with me please:

   - Phone me on +441234 56789
   - Contact me via LinkedIn.

6. Preferred pronouns. These are especially useful in the diverse, multigender world in which we live and/or if you have a name which could be male or female. Typical examples are:

| Identity | Preferred pronouns |
|---|---|
| Male | He/him/his |
| Female | She/her/hers |
| Gender neutral or not wanting to identify with a specific gender | They/them/theirs |

7. Awards. Special awards from global to company-specific.

8. *A head and shoulders photo of yourself* – This is becoming increasingly common.

## Multiple Different Signatures

In Microsoft Outlook and Gmail, you can have different signatures for internal and external messages and the first and subsequent email messages. Again, you may have no choice, but where you do, make full use of this functionality.

### *Windows Microsoft Outlook*

1. Go to File/Options/Mail.

2. In the Mail dialogue box, and under Compose messages, click on Signatures.

3. To create a new signature, click on New and give it a name. Click OK. Complete the E-mail Signature dialogue box as shown below, choosing the words, font, etc.

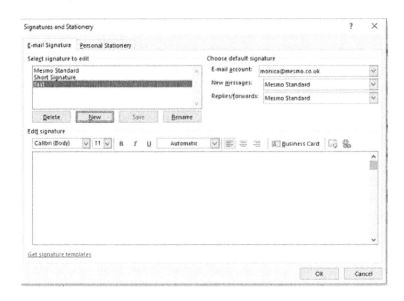

4. To add your preferred social media icons, click on the image button (under Edit signature second from end at right) and choose the image from the appropriate file (using the Insert image finder box as shown below).

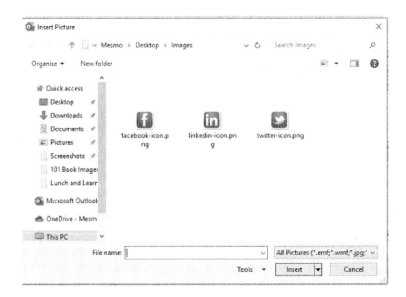

5. To hyperlink the icon to your site, click on the icon and then the Hyperlink icon (next to the Image button).

6. At this point, select one of your signatures as the default. Then click on OK when you have finished.

7. To change which signature you use when you compose / reply to a message, from the Include block on the Home tab, click on Signatures and choose from the list you have saved.

## Mac Outlook 365

1. Go to Outlook/Preferences and select Signatures. Use the dialogue box below to compile your signatures.

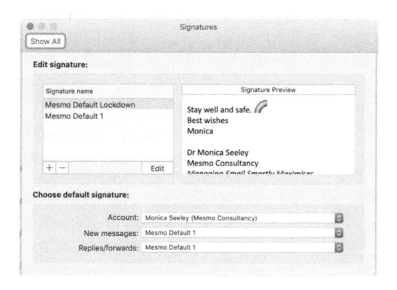

2. Click on + and a new signature box opens up for you to complete. Use the Signature box shown below to add the text, social media icons and images of awards and to hyperlink the icons.

## Gmail

To create multiple signatures, from the Settings gear, click All Settings. Scroll down to 'Signature' and click 'Create New' to create additional signatures. To use a different signature in a message, open the Insert signature menu (pen icon).

**Pro Tip:**

If you do shorten the signature after the first message, your contact phone number is still the one item you should include. Why? After three rounds of email message ping-pong, this might be when the recipient would really like to speak to you. However, if it is not instantly obvious, the moment will pass, and you'll go on communicating by email messages when a phone call would have been so much more productive.

# | Tip #13 |

## Dealing With Language Barriers

*Messages lost in translation can negatively impact businesses*
*by hampering international deals.*
*– Economist Intelligence Unit 2012*

## The Challenge

Not surprisingly, many PAs and EAs who work for global organisations ask for tips to help them communicate as clearly as possible through an email message to others for whom English is not their mother tongue. They want to limit not only the risk of a misunderstanding, but also the rounds of email ping-pong because the original message needed further clarification.

## The Solution

There are several factors to consider, such as how to structure the email; and the actual words you use, especially those with double meaning (homonyms), and those where the pronunciation is the same but the spelling is different depending on the context within which they are used (homophones). Technology can help.

## Content

The golden rules are: firstly, keep the content as short as possible. Remember email messages are what they say, messages. Secondly, imagine yourself as the recipient and how you would feel receiving the message. For example, given the Covid-19 pandemic, what is the recipient's working environment: kitchen table at home, back in the office but perhaps stressed after travelling on public transport? Here are 10 top tips for the content.

1. Structure the content so that it flows and there is a beginning, middle and end. Sometimes this means re-reading and editing your message before you hit send. This is always time well spent.

2. Keep it succinct – Think five: five sentences, five bullet points, five paragraphs.

3. Run a spelling and grammar check before sending and make sure that the spell checker has not changed the context and meaning of a word.

4. Avoid colloquialisms, local jargon and jokes. These rarely translate well into other languages and can leave the recipient confused or even offended.

5. Limit the use of emoticons. Although they are widely understood and do translate, there are other downsides. See Tip 11, 'Email Etiquette: Text vs. Emoticons', page 34.

6. Be polite, kind and considerate. For example, don't just ask for a report by a certain time. Preface your request with a compliment, such as 'Thank you for your previous hard work; is it possible to have your report by Thursday so that my executive does not miss their deadline?'

7. Use simple rather than complex words. For instance, instead of 'assignment' maybe use 'project' or 'task'.

8. Be factual and not emotional, objective not subjective.

9. If the message is long (five paragraphs) provide an overview (like an executive summary) at the beginning of the message, outlining what it is about. This is especially useful for those reading their messages on a mobile device.

10. Grammar and punctuation matter and play an important part in helping the other person understand. See Tip 6, 'Punctuation Is Important', page 14.

For more details on the best ways to write the content of an email, see 'The Executive Secretary Guide to Taking Control of Your Inbox'.

## Homonyms and homophones

Below is a list of some of the more common examples, reproduced with kind permission of Marcham Publishing from 'The Executive Secretary' Guide to Taking Control of Your Inbox'.

| Homonyms | Homophones |
|---|---|
| Leaves | Buy/Bye/By |
| Foil | Morning/Mourning |
| Point | Their/There |
| Net | Principal/Principle |
| Rose | Grate/Great |
| Bow | Hail/Hale |

To help the recipient and hence save time, either find a replacement word or add an explanation. For instance, write 'rose (the flower)', while 'buy' could be replaced with 'purchase'. 'Point' meaning an item in a list could be replaced with a number, while 'point' meaning the reason for the meeting could be replaced by 'purpose'.

## *Technology to help overcome language barriers*

While current technology has still not quite reached Douglas Adams's Babel Fish levels of translation (in 'The Hitchhiker's Guide to the Galaxy'), here are four ways technology can help.

1. Translation tools. Try translating your message into the other person's first language. Both Microsoft Word and Google Docs have built-in translation functions. In Word, it is located in the Review toolbar. You can copy the text of your email message to a Word document and use it. Then copy the translated text back into the message. Alternatively, and especially if you are using a mobile device, use one of the translation tools/apps such as Google Translate, iTranslate, or Microsoft Translator. In Google Docs, click the Tools dropdown menu and select Translate.

*A word of caution about translation tools: Often you will get a readable translation that isn't exactly correct or appropriate, but you won't know it. If you can't validate it with someone who speaks the language, and the nature of your message might be one that implies a contract or transaction, ensure that you are clear that the message is not intended for that purpose.*

2. Common Words. Learn some common words in the other person's language, again using one of the freely available apps such as Duolingo.

3. Translation software. There are a number of enterprise level translation software systems. They are not cheap, but most offer a free trial. You may find your organisation already has such software if it is a large global business. Typical users might be the legal and procurement departments who need to translate large documents.

4. Readability score. Based on the American Flesch-Kincaid readability test, this score rates how easy it is for someone to read your text. Scores range from 10 to 100. The higher the number, the easier it is to read. A good score is between 60 and

70, which means it is easy for a 13-year-old (based on an American level of education).

Microsoft Word has a Readability function, but you must activate it. Go to Preferences/Spelling and Grammar and tick the Readability box as shown below. In Google Docs, search the Add-ons for available Flesch-Kincaid readability tools developed for G Suite.

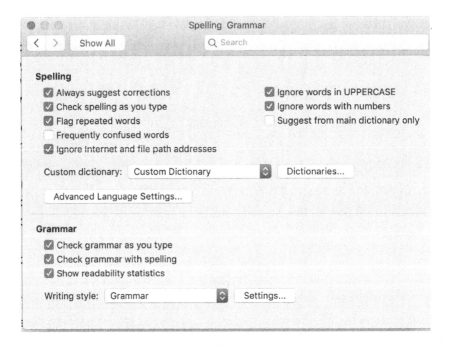

To use the Readability statistics, again paste the text into a Word document and use the Spelling and Grammar function (from the Review toolbox). Once complete, click on OK and the statistics are provided as shown below.

| Readability Statistics | |
|---|---|
| **Counts** | |
| Words | 520 |
| Characters | 2,842 |
| Paragraphs | 25 |
| Sentences | 38 |
| **Averages** | |
| Sentences per Paragraph | 2.2 |
| Words per Sentence | 12.7 |
| Characters per Word | 4.5 |
| **Readability** | |
| Flesch Reading Ease | 65.8 |
| Flesch-Kincaid Grade Level | 7.1 |
| Passive Sentences | 5.2% |
| | OK |

## *Ask for feedback to keep improving your performance*

If you are on the receiving end of email messages written by a sender whose native language is not English, you can always suggest they write in their first language and you make the translation. Remember too that most apps will also translate text to speech, which can be helpful.

- Being successful means adopting the lifelong learning mantra. Make sure you ask for feedback when you do send messages to those with whom there may be a language difference; so that you can try to reduce the gap over time.

# Tip #14

## What You Say When You Say Nothing: Is It OK to NOT Respond to Email?

## The Challenge

Here is an interesting question which an EA recently posed during a webinar. 'Last week I received an email from a colleague which I did not feel warranted a reply. Is it OK to say nothing and hence not reply?'

## The Solution

You are the owner of your time. If you don't manage it, then others will do so by making demands on it which either are unreasonable or mean you have to change your priorities for the day. Clearly if it is your manager, then you may need to say 'yes, but' and renegotiate priorities. If it's a colleague, you have more scope to say 'no, not at the moment', in the politest possible way.

Email messages are the biggest source of time-wasters. It is easy for people to fire off new messages and responses without a moment's thought about the impact on you and your time. Not replying to colleagues' messages is a very vexed question. On the one hand, it may send a signal that you are too busy,; on the other hand, to not even acknowledge the message may be considered rude. Some might even see you as inefficient.

Imagine you are walking along a corridor and do not make eye contact with one person but go boldly up to the next one and engage. How might the first person feel?

On balance, you should respond in some way to most work-related email messages. The question then is within what time-scales and how, especially if the sender is making unjustifiable demands on your time, was rude or does not know when to stop a discussion.

Here are eight classic messages to which you may choose either to delay a reply or respond by politely saying 'no'.

*Email messages you may choose either to ignore or say 'no' to-*

| | Type of email | Potential response |
|---|---|---|
| 1 | Rude | No email response. Instead call the sender to <u>ask</u> 'what is the problem'? |
| 2 | Making a demand on your time which you either cannot or do not wish to undertake | Be assertive and explain that much as you might like to help, you have other priorities/demands on your time. Make sure you <u>don't</u> leave open the door for the person to come back later! |
| 3 | Jokes and gossip | Ignore these. However, if you feel they are in poor taste and may cause a problem with others, a gentle warning via a phone call might be a good idea. |
| 4 | CC emails | Typically, these do not require a response. Remember the golden rule, cc is for information only. Either ask to have yourself taken off the |

## *What is an acceptable response time?*

There is no hard and fast rule. Between 24 and 48 hours is a good baseline. Clearly, much depends on the sender and how close to the front-line you are. The more important the sender is to you and the nearer the frontline of the business, the shorter the response time.

Much outside 48 hours and there is good chance the sender will resend their message and thus drive up the email message traffic.

If you cannot respond within 48 hours, then at least send a holding response managing the sender's expectation about when you can take action. This is especially good when you are juggling your inbox on the road. See Tip 45, 'Juggling the Inbox on the Road', page 154.

# ‖ Tip #15 ‖

## Communicating Urgent

## The Challenge

Received from an executive assistant: 'I look after my executive's inbox. Most days he spends at least three quarters of his day in meetings (face-to-face or virtual). He has a mobile device and dips in and out between meetings looking for anything which he feels needs his attention quickly such as those from the CEO. We are a global organisation, which means email messages come in early in the morning and late at night. Often there are urgent messages which need a response from him within a specific time frame because of the different time zones within which we operate. We have tried various options for me to draw his attention to these items such as flags and folders. However, because of the volume of email messages, it is easy for them to get overlooked. What options do you suggest for communicating the urgency of such messages?'

## The Solution

This is one of the most common problems faced by PAs and EAs who support senior executives. There is not one best process for indicating 'urgent'. The optimum process depends on what the executive perceives as urgent at any one time, with what technology they are comfortable, the device they use and whether or not they stick to the agreed process. Here is a selection of techniques that other PAs and EAs use ranging from email messages to WhatsApp alerts.

## Email Messages

There are four principle ways to use the inbox to alert your executive to urgent messages which they need to respond to as quickly as possible.

1. *'Urgent' in the subject line* – Edit the subject line and add the word URGENT. Add a date and time if relevant. See Tip 39, 'Editing an Email to Show the Action Taken', page 137.

2. *Flags* – Add a follow-up flag and, if necessary, set a reminder date for the previous day so that it goes red in their inbox. See Tip 52, 'Flags or Tasks for Reminder?', page 184, for more on this.

3. *Create an Urgent folder* – Start it with either a full stop or dash and it will sit at the top of the inbox folder list. Place all such email messages in there and add a comment about what action your executive needs to take.

4. *Categories* – Define a category and add it to the message. You can only use categories on your executive's messages if you are logged in to your executive's inbox as them or have Owner level permission.

The major disadvantage of any inbox-related process is that the executive will be distracted by another message that they decide to answer and then forget to check their Urgent folder.

## WhatsApp or Text

Many use WhatsApp or other text message platforms to tell their executive about very urgent messages that need their attention. The advantages of this approach are that it is quick and easy, conveys a sense of urgency and can be seen discretly during a meeting.

## Phone

Yes, some still use the more traditional way of a simple phone call. The disadvantage is that it is not always acceptable if your phone goes off during a meeting.

## The Choice Is Yours

Which one you choose depends entirely on your situation, how you work together; and your executive's preference. Also remember, what is in the inbox and how you handle it is a picture of you. This applies to your executive too. Some are fundamentally well-organised and like the Urgent folder method and go straight there.

Others with a more serendipitous *modus operandi* will be the ones who dip in and out of the inbox and deal with what they feel is relevant at that moment. For example, they may have a network of critical key contacts. An email message from any one of these will take priority over anything else, as they know it's from a highly trusted colleague and may contain exceptionally valuable information, such as an early warning of a new competitor.

You may need to pilot several processes before you find the one which works best for you both. Sometimes if nothing really works well for the pair of you, you just have to resort to constant reminders in the nicest possible way – assuring the executive that you are doing it as their best friend watching out for them!

# MANAGEABLE EMAIL

# ‖ Tip #16 ‖

## The Inbox Highway – See the Wood for the Trees in a Cluttered Inbox

### The Challenge

With a daily tsunami of 50+ email messages arriving each day, it's very easy to miss that all-important one. An important email now becomes Important + Urgent, which equals stress. This could be an email from either a key client or a member of the organisation.

### The Solution

There is a very easy and simple way to reduce the risk of missing important email. Treat your inbox as an information highway. You decide what traffic, in this case email, travels in the fast lane straight to the inbox and what travels in the slow lane via folder for you to read later. Here are three easy steps to de-clutter your inbox.

1.  Prioritise each incoming email. Review each incoming email over say a period of 3 to 5 days and give it a priority:

    -   H = Very important, must see within the next two to six hours.

    -   M = Important but could wait for a day or two before it needs my attention.

- L = Not important, maybe even do not need to see this email.

The timescales should be adjusted to fit your role and needs. For example, Very Important might mean you need to see it immediately.

2. Decide where the email arrives. Does the message travel in the fast lane straight to your inbox or the slow lane to a folder?
3. Use rules to police your email highway. For all those email messages which do not need to travel in the fast lane, write a rule to send them to the slow lane, directly to a folder. These messages can be of any priority, from H to L. Indeed, for the low priority email the folder might just be 'Deleted Items'. You never wanted them in the first place, but for whatever reason you are unable to take yourself off the distribution list.

Now the question is, what's the quickest way to see all the unread email without trawling through multiple folders?

Answer – use the smart Search Folders which sit at the bottom of your inbox. You can even add it to Favourites to keep it at the top of your Navigation Pane.

⌄ Favorites

_CAPSTONE2020

| | |
|---|---|
| Unread Mail | **493** |
| Today | **2** |
| Sent Directly to Me | **6** |

# ‖ Tip #17 ‖

## Inbox Zero – Is It a Good Idea?

### The Challenge

I've heard people talk about inbox zero. What is it and is it worth setting it as a goal?

## Inbox Zero – The Basic Concept

The term was coined in 2004 by Merlin Mann, a productivity guru. It was part of his '43 Folders' process to free up time to do your creative work and not be distracted. In essence, you action the important email messages and delete the rest. Once you have dealt with an email, you move it out of your inbox either into a folder for no further action or one of the 43 tickler files (reminder folder), 43 being the number of working days; thus, each folder represents a working day on which the email is to be brought forward. Mann later simplified the number to five folders:

- **Delete** – Including archiving email messages you may have read and want to keep.
- **Delegate** – Forward the email to a colleague who can help/ action the email messages as the term infers.
- **Respond** – If you can reply within two minutes, do so. If it's going to take longer move it to the Defer folder.

- **Action** – Do what you are asked now.

His process gained prominence after he gave a presentation to Google. It can still be found on YouTube;, look up 'Merlin Mann Inbox Zero'. It was invented just before mobile devices and Gmail exploded onto the scene. Volumes of email were about 50% less than now. Nonetheless, the concept of inbox zero is still a holy grail, although even Mann himself admits that it is not the most productive use of your time.

## Inbox Zero – The Positive Side

- Achieving inbox zero assumes you move email messages out of your inbox after actioning them.
- It plays to an emotional sense of self-gratification and achievement – today, I've dealt with all my email messages.
- It helps reduce the stress of an overflowing inbox on the basis that out of sight is out of mind, assuming you can either find the email messages later on or have a robust process for bringing them back if they still need attention.
- You become ruthless at not answering email messages which are either low priority or unnecessary because you delete them.
- You can improve GDRP compliance, as it is easier to manage/housekeep a small folder rather than a large one.
- It appeals to people who like a tidy desk.

## Inbox Zero – The Downside

- You spend too much time clearing the inbox instead of dealing with more important tasks, e.g. another sales call.
- You can easily lose sight of the thread of an email conversation.
- It's easy to be distracted by new incoming email messages in your eagerness to keep the inbox at zero.
- You may miss an important email in the haste to delete.

- It can become an obsession which leads to addictive behaviour.
- Inbox zero will not work for those who are happier working with a messy desk.

## The Solution

A *clean inbox* rather than inbox zero is the approach we favour. Remove all the unnecessary email messages either manually or (preferably) using rules/ filters (see Tip 46, 'Rules Rule, Gmail Filters', page 160). However, accept that some days it will be hard to deal with all your email messages. Working late into the night to reach inbox zero will leave its imprint on your productivity the next day. If you see your inbox as a work in progress, then it is acceptable to have a few email messages which still need your attention.

With large inbox capacity now the norm and with powerful fast search functions, some have now coined the phrase 'inbox infinity' to counter the inbox zero concept: just leave everything in the main inbox.

At the end of the day, the key to improving your performance is having a reliable process which works for you and your personality and role. While some processes are more efficient and some more likely to breach GDPR than others, you must choose whether or not making a change is worth the investment of your time because change does not happen overnight.

The critical factor to improving your productivity is to ensure that once you open/read an email you do something with it and don't just leave it lying in your inbox to be re-read again. See Tip 34, 'Handle Each Email Only Once – The 4Ds Principle', page 120.

# Tip #18

## Managing Conversations in Outlook

## The Challenge

Finding needles in haystacks is a concept that appears multiple times in this book. It is a common and consistent challenge when it comes to large volumes of email. One solution to the haystack is Conversation View in Outlook.

Since Office 2010, Microsoft Outlook has offered the choice of viewing your email messages by conversation. However, even people who have both Gmail and Outlook have chafed at the idea of seeing their email messages in Outlook organised by conversation. It may be because if you can't see it right in front of you, it might not be there (though most of us don't have a challenge with object permanence in other aspects of our lives). Once you know how it really works, you'll find many uses for it both as a temporary working view or a permanent way of viewing your messages.

## The Solution

What is Conversation View?

If you remember the older term 'discussion thread' you already know the intent of Conversation View. What Gmail has done for ages and what Outlook does now is provide you a look at an entire thread or conversation, including related messages stored in places other than your inbox, plus your responses, in a nice neat list. Initially, all messages within a conversation appear collapsed to one item. You'll notice little right-pointing white arrows to the left that allow you to expand and collapse each one. Message listings are formatted depending upon whether they are read or **unread**, and from someone or *from you*.

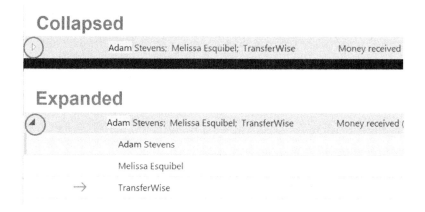

## How Do You Set It Up?

1. Be sure your messages are sorted by date. It does not matter if they are grouped (Today, Yesterday, Last Week) or not.

2. On the View tab, click the 'Show as Conversations' check box. Respond All Folders or All Mailboxes. (This same operation works to remove Conversation View).

3. Look for the white arrows and click to expand. At times, this operation may seem not to work. Be sure before you click that the arrow changes colour when you hover over it. Then, click slightly to the right.

4. If the arrow remains white after expanding, it indicates that this is a 'split thread' meaning that some responses were made to different messages in the thread. Repeat Step 3 until you see the whole thread.

## What Tools Does It Offer?

You get two nifty tools with Conversation View. Clean Up allows you to remove redundant messages. Wait! REMOVE MESSAGES? Yes, but only those that are truly redundant. That means that the message in its entirety is included inside another email message. Any messages that contain attachments or which change something about the body of the message or subject will be kept individually, yet still remain part of the conversation. This reduces the number of messages you must read to stay up to date with what has occurred since the last time you read messages in the thread. Simply run Clean Up, then start reading at the bottom-most unread message.

Ignore Conversation is useful for messages from people you want to hear from about things you don't want to hear about. For example, a colleague sends you an email with pictures of her newborn kittens. Instantly, email starts cluttering your inbox, both about loving the pictures and wanting to get off the mailing list. You still need to get important messages from this colleague, but don't have time to keep deleting the kitten mail. By ignoring a selected conversation, you've essentially written a rule that routes messages in that conversation directly to the Deleted Items folder.

Fair warning, though; if you regularly communicate with people who don't stay on subject, you might miss a few things that could be important. Help educate your wayward communicators by clipping anything off-topic and creating a new email message to them with something like the following:

'I was concerned this might get missed. Created a new message for you to send to whoever you like to start a new discussion of this important topic.'

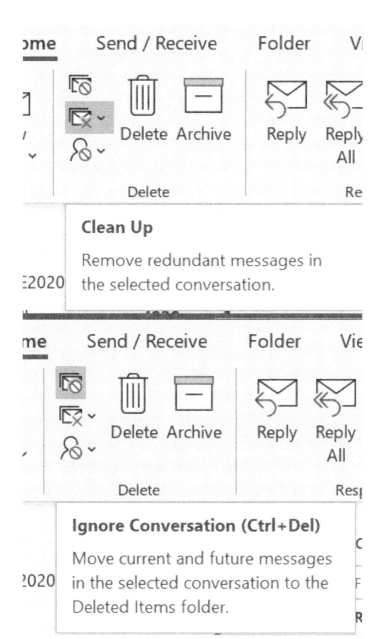

# ‖ Tip #19 ‖

## Outlook: Shift+Delete

## The Challenge

If you look in your Deleted Items folder, you'll recognise messages that fit into two categories: 'Maybe I don't need this' and 'Definitely I don't need this'. In fact, I'll venture to say at least half of the items are in the latter category.

There are a few different ways of handling the Deleted Items folder. Some clear it on some sort of regular schedule, such as daily or weekly. Others maintain the items they've deleted until they're forced to clear them by hitting account size limits. I've even heard of someone who's actually created folders in Deleted Items. (The image I get in my mind is that of someone leaning over their rubbish bin, filing.)

## The Solution

Best practices say you should empty Deleted Items daily. If the thought of that worries you, ask why you deleted these items in the first place. While you are pondering whether you are strong enough to right-click on Deleted Items and select Empty Folder, here's a new practice to get into that will ultimately make the task easier: Use Shift +Delete to permanently delete items you know you don't need.

Maybe you're a little concerned about deleting that email about how to properly shake hands with a client, because one day you think you might be doing that again. But consider the spam message that escaped through your spam and junk filters; about pharmaceutical products you don't need and which are from a country you've never heard of. That one you know you don't need? Shift+Delete it! Now, it's gone-gone. It is not in Deleted Items, it's nowhere.

By not filling up Deleted Items with things you know you don't need, you will better be able to see those items which perhaps need to be retrieved from the bin and filed elsewhere. By the way, Shift+Delete also works well on selections of items, so if you sort by From and decide that the 20 items sent to you from this one address fit the description 'Definitely I don't need', Shift+Del from the grouping to permanently delete them all.

---

**Pro Tip:**

For the items you think you might need one day, why not save them (or the link to the news item) in an electronic notebook like OneNote?

---

# ‖ Tip #20 ‖

## Using Retention Periods in Outlook

Microsoft offers several tools to help you keep your inbox and folders clean. One that has been used for decades is the Archive folder. Another more recent one is the ability to set a retention policy. In this case, whether automatically by a rule or manually as you decide, an email message can be moved out of your inbox. Generally speaking, it remains retrievable for a period of time; and is then removed based on policies set by the Exchange administrator.

## The Challenge

The most attended webinars of modern times always include the words 'inbox clean-up' in the titles'. Especially popular at the beginning of the year, this rarely fails to attract a good crowd. Why? Because keeping the inbox manageable is a perpetual challenge and because many Outlook users don't know all the tools available to them to help them meet it. Hitting the delete key is effective (Shift +Delete even more so), but not as effective as having Outlook take care of binning messages automatically.

Many people set up rules to automatically move unwanted messages to the Deleted Items folder. Some messages are those not caught by our organisation's spam filters and some are from 'friendlies' writing to us about things we are not interested in. There are several reasons why automatically sending these to Deleted Items might cause us to miss items they send us that we actually are interested in. Sure, we can scan Deleted Items from time to time before we empty it to see if we might have missed anything, but this is truly a needle in a haystack exercise.

## The Solution

Attaching retention policies to selected messages is an 'in between' type of solution. We can move an item to a folder called 'Newsletters' and set up a retention period of 30 days, especially in the case of a monthly update. The newsletters or 'needles' are then kept in a place called 'needle box' rather than thrown into a bin with absolutely everything else we delete. So, how does it work?

### How It Works

Typically, Outlook makes available some preset retention policies for us to choose from.

- 1 Month Delete (30 days)
- 1 Week Delete
- 1 Year Delete
- 5 Year Delete
- 6 Month Delete
- Never Delete

Your organisation may have already set up additional retention policies and made some decisions around what happens to an email on which a policy has been set. To set a policy on a single email message, right-click the message line and choose Assign Policy. When you are presented with the list, choose the appropriate one. That's it! Once the retention period has come and gone, the message will be moved to a predetermined place, where you may retrieve it if necessary. To recover it, click on the Folder tab (Outlook desktop) and then the Recover Deleted Items button.

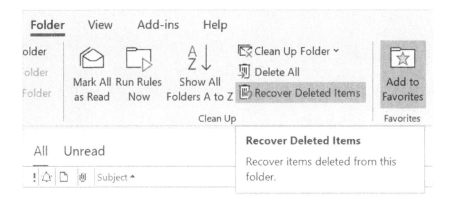

Check with your IT staff to determine how long messages are kept available here and, if possible, other retention periods that might be useful for you to be able to set.

## Applying Retention Policies With a Rule

To use this feature in a rule:

1. Right-click on any email message and choose Rules – Create Rule.
2. Then, click on the Advanced button in the lower right corner of the dialogue box.
3. Select the criteria that would apply, such as from a specific email address or with specific words in the subject or body (see Tip 23, 'Outlook Rules Rule!', page 81, for more tips on writing rules). Click Next.
4. On this part of the rule dialogue, scroll to the bottom of the available actions and check 'Apply retention policy.'
5. In the Step 2 box at the bottom, click 'Retention policy' and select one.

Rules Wizard

What do you want to do with the message?
Step 1: Select action(s)

- ☐ permanently delete it
- ☐ move a copy to the specified folder
- ☐ forward it to people or public group
- ☐ forward it to people or public group as an attachment
- ☐ redirect it to people or public group
- ☐ have server reply using a specific message
- ☐ reply using a specific template
- ☐ flag message for follow up at this time
- ☐ clear the Message Flag
- ☐ clear message's categories
- ☐ mark it as importance
- ☐ print it
- ☐ play a sound
- ☐ mark it as read
- ☐ stop processing more rules
- ☐ display a specific message in the New Item Alert window
- ☐ display a Desktop Alert
- ☑ apply retention policy: retention policy

Step 2: Edit the rule description (click an underlined value)

Apply this rule after the message arrives
with Power Automate – Newsletter in the subject
apply retention policy: retention policy

From now on, messages with that criteria will automatically be assigned that retention period. You can also add an action step here to put it into a particular folder. Both actions will happen at the same time.

## Applying Retention Policies to a Folder

Retention policies can also be set on folders. To do this:

- Right-click the folder and select Properties.
- Click the Policy card at the top.
- Change Use the Parent Folder Policy to one of the selections that appear in the dropdown list.

If you have set up a Quick Step or a rule to automatically move items to this folder, it will automatically apply that retention period.

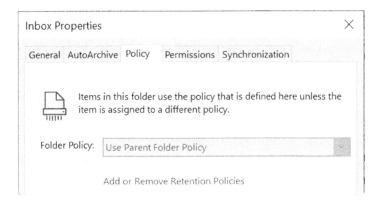

---

### Pro Tip:

If you're concerned about items coming to the end of their retention periods, right-click any message and choose Assign Policy, then View Items Expiring Soon.

---

# ‖ Tip #21 ‖

## Conditional Formatting

This is a term that has been used for many years in Microsoft Excel, and with the release of Outlook 2010, it became how we referred to the feature in Outlook that allows us to specify conditions under which an email will appear in a view in a different colour.

## The Challenge

How do you easily spot important email messages as they arrive in your inbox? You can customise rules to apply conditional formatting to certain messages. For example, if you support four different executives or are working on four different projects, you can easily spot who they are from and/or what they are about without even reading the line item in your inbox!

## The Solution

There is already some conditional formatting at play in Outlook by default. For example, your unread items show up bold in the inbox. Items to which you have applied follow-up flags and which are now past due appear in the view in red text.

You can specify your own special formatting for email messages, meeting criteria such as from a specific person, about a particular subject or with certain contents in the body.

Let's take the example of colour-coding email messages from a particular person.

1.  If the person's email address is in your Contacts, you're all set to begin. Otherwise, copy it from an email you received or create a contact from that email message by dragging it to the contacts icon or the word People in the bottom navigation area.
2.  On the View tab in the Current View group, click the View Settings button.
3.  Choose Conditional Formatting from the dialogue box that appears.
4.  Click Add.
5.  Complete the Name field.
6.  Click the Font... button and select the formatting you prefer for this condition.
7.  Click the Condition... button and either paste the email address you copied into the From... field or click the From... button and select the right name from your Contacts. (While you are here, take a look around at all the different ways you can specify conditions.)
8.  Click OK. You should notice that the messages meeting the criteria you specified show up in that format.

Keep in mind that conditional formatting attaches to that view. When you change the view, you may not see the same formatting. You would need to apply it to each view in which you'd like to see it.

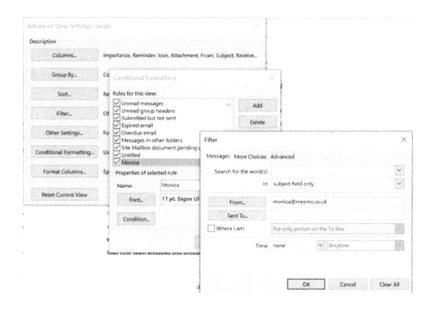

# | Tip #22 |

## Creating Categories in Outlook

## The Challenge

While most Outlook users are using folders to organise everything from email messages to contacts, it is sometimes necessary to create a level of organisation that can be seen within a folder. A growing number of Outlook users have abandoned folders altogether and have chosen instead to organise everything by categories. How can you put this technique to work for you?

## The Solution

Folders are fine, but categories can offer another way or another level of organisation in email messages, calendars, contacts, tasks and more. Here are a few ways categories are used.

- Differentiate types of meetings on the calendar, such as Internal, Client, Board and Interview.
- Group tasks by project so they all can appear in the main task folder and be sorted to provide an overall list of projects and their associated tasks.
- Group contacts by client, where you have more than one per client.

- Cluster email by action type within a folder. For example, you have several email messages from a single client in various stages of completion or closure (pending approval, need to call, send proposal).

## Finding the Categorize Button

### *Ribbon*

The great thing about categories is that you'll find where to create them from where you need to create them. The Categorize button appears in the Home tab, in the Tags group when in the following views: Email (Mail), Contacts (People) and Tasks.

### *In an item*

You won't see it on Calendar in the Home tab. However, from inside any Calendar item, you'll see it on the Meeting or Appointment tab, which is in the same position as where the Home tab would be on the far left. This also applies to Task items, Contacts and Messages.

### *Right-click menu*

You can also right-click any item and see the Categorize button on the menu. Just hover over the menu item and the fly-out menu will reveal the available categories. Just select one and you're done!

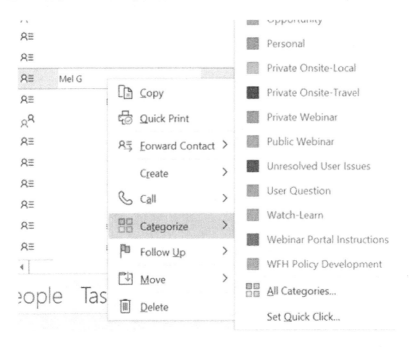

## Creating a New Category

If you've never created a category, you'll see something like Red Category, Blue Category, Yellow Category and so on. If you do see some, but not the one you need, look for it by clicking the All Categories selection from either the right-click menu or from the drop down button on the ribbon. From the colour Categories dialogue, you might see a longer list of categories.

If you still don't have the one you need, you can select one of the generic ones (for example, Red Category) and click the Rename button. From there just type the new name. If you need a brand new one, click the New button. Give it a name. Choose a colour. And, if you'd like to be able to categorize from a shortcut key combination, click the dropdown next to that field. You'll be able to choose from Ctrl+F2 to Ctrl+F12. There are 25 colours to choose from with the option to also choose None. Colours can be reused. The important thing is the name. So, you might have a Red Category indicate a client meeting and another Red Category mean 'Need to Call' on an email message.

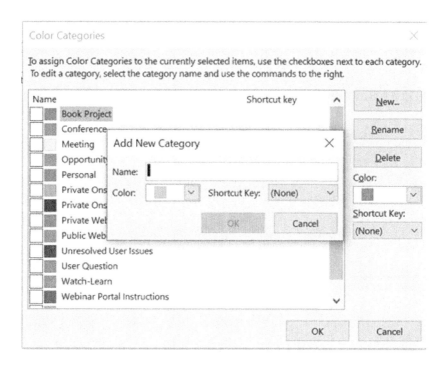

One more place you'll see categories is in the various views of each group of items. By default, it is usually on the right. You can right-click the little box that appears there to choose a category, too.

Here's a cool trick to see a collapsed view of items by category, from which you could expand just one or two. For example, expand your email messages that require phone calls when you're at your best during the day. Then make your calls!

1. Click the Categories column header in the view to sort. Then click it again. This will put any non-categorized items at the bottom.

2. In the View tab, click the Expand/Collapse button and choose Collapse All Groups.

3. Expand the ones you want to see in detail by clicking the > button to the left of the high-level grouping.

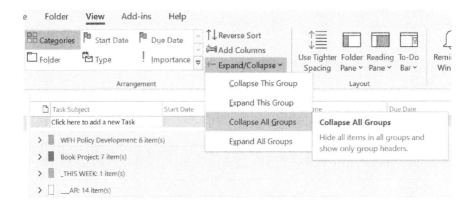

# Tip #23

## Outlook Rules Rule!

## The Challenge

You've set up your folder structure, your categories and overall organisational strategy. But addressing each item manually can be tedious and time-consuming.

## The Solution

Automate the process with rules. A rule examines the email item for criteria you define, then takes an action. They can automatically categorize, folder, forward, flag and even delete an email when it first comes in! Let's say we'd like to have all email from a particular company go into a certain folder. We want it to remain showing as unread, but we don't want it to stay in the main inbox. If we're on the road, we also want the email to go to our assistant or colleague. Rules even allow you to specify exceptions. For example, send all email messages with the word Newsletter in the subject line to a folder called 'Read Later', unless it's coming from a close colleague whose job it is to alert you of anything newsworthy that you should take action on. Here's how it works.

## Setting Up a Rule

From the Home tab, find the Move Group, Rules button, then Create Rule. You'll start from a basic rule dialogue box which allows you to specify any or all of the following criteria:

- From a particular user.
- With a subject line that has certain text.
- That has been sent to a particular email account.

You can then take the following actions:

- Display in the New Item Alert window.
- Play a selected sound.
- Move to a folder.

To do more with your rules, click on the Advanced Options button. Let's say we need a rule that folders all email messages from anyone whose email address is from a certain domain, such as mesmo.co.uk.

1. In the first dialogue we'll check 'with specific words in the sender's address'.
2. To specify the company's email domain, click 'specific words' in the bottom part of the dialogue which shows the rules script.
3. Type the domain then click the Add button. In this way, the rule will apply no matter who is writing to me from mesmo.co.uk.
4. Click OK and Next.
5. On the next screen, check 'move it to the specified folder".
6. Click on the hyperlink on the bottom that says 'specified' in the bottom part of the dialogue.
7. On the next dialogue box, find the folder you have set up for that company, or create it from here by clicking on the New button.
8. You could also click 'forward it to people or distribution list' and specify an assistant or colleague who is your back-up with that client.

9.  On the next screen you can specify exceptions to the rule if needed.

10. Click Finish.

11. On the last screen, you can decide to run the rules on everything you already have in your inbox or just turn it on to run the next time mail comes in.

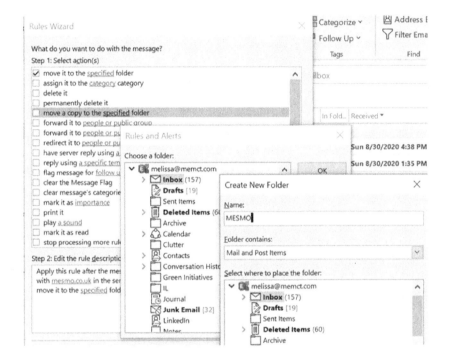

## Gotchas

Rules will run in the order in which they are stored. Click on the Rules button again and choose Manage Rules and Alerts to see the list and the order in which they'll run. You'll see the words 'and stop processing more rules' at the bottom if that applies. This is where the order is important. If you want an email message to be subject to more than just one rule, one which is marked to stop processing more rules will cause the other rules to be ignored.

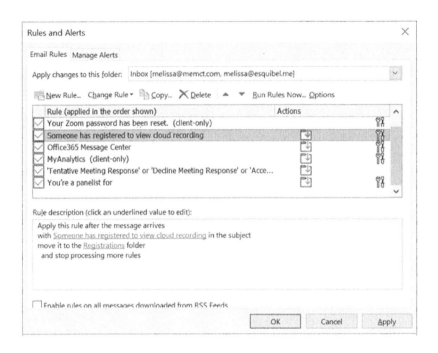

Another 'gotcha' is that some rules will run on the Exchange server whether or not you have Outlook open (applies to on-premise Exchange servers and Office 365 cloud-based Exchange). Others will only run if you've opened Outlook on your computer. If you set up a rule like the latter, you will get a message as you close the Rules dialogue boxes.

## What Else Can I Do?

From the dialogue box you just visited (Manage Rules and Alerts), you could click on the New Rule button and actually write a rule for messages you send. For example, set up a rule which looks for a predetermined subject line text string like 'ABC Invoice #.' Then have it set a follow-up flag in an advanced rule for 30 days with a reminder. That way you'll be alerted to the payment due and can remove the flag if payment was received.

And there's so much more! Explore all the options and see where you can put Outlook on autopilot and reduce the tedium of managing email that rules can manage for you.

# Tip #24

## Sweep Meeting Responses

## The Challenge

In an effort to keep your inbox tidy, you can remove messages that are Meeting Accept, Decline, or Tentative Accept items. Some hesitate to do this as they assume that the meeting tracking information stored for the meeting item will be affected. In fact, the tracking information is impacted by the responder's email action item when it is received. However, after that, it is no longer needed. Here is a technique that you can use, or use in modified form, to sequester those email messages off to a temporary folder, which you can 'sweep' or clean up on a regular, perhaps daily basis.

## The Solution

In the following process we will set up a filtering rule in Outlook (desktop versions for PC 2010 and later) to catch all messages that are using the forms Accept Meeting Response, Decline Meeting Response and Tentative Meeting Response and folder them. We will even set up an exception to route messages that have additional information from the responder to your inbox for your review.

1.  On the Home tab in the Move group, click the Rules button.

2. Choose Create Rule.

3. In the Create Rule dialogue, click the Advanced Options button in the lower right corner.

4. In the Step 1: Select condition(s) dialogue, locate 'Uses the form name form' near the bottom part of the list and check the box.

5. In the lower part of the dialogue box you will see the form name hyperlink. Click it.

6. In the Choose Forms dialogue, change Personal Forms to Application Forms in the top left field by clicking the dropdown arrow.

7. In the list of forms below, double click the following selections: Accept Meeting Response, Decline Meeting Response and Tentative Meeting Response. You may also select them by holding down the Ctrl key and click Add. Either method will get them to the right side of the dialogue under Selected forms.

8. Click the Close button at the bottom.

9. Back on the Rules Wizard dialogue, click the Next button at the bottom.

10. In the Step 1: Select actions(s) dialogue, choose the first option: move it to the specified folder.

11. In the lower part of the dialogue box, click the specified hyperlink.

12. Click the New button on the right and create the folder in which you want to temporarily store these items. OPTION: you can also choose to delete it or permanently delete it instead of move it to the specified folder if you do not need to review them before sweeping them.

13. Back on the Rules Wizard dialogue, click the Next button at the bottom.

14. On the Step 1: Select exception(s) (if necessary), locate and check the box next to 'except where the body contains specific words'.

15. In the lower part of the dialogue box, click the specific words hyperlink.

16. In succession, type the letter a in the top field and click the Add button, followed by e, i, o, u and y. This should catch most messages someone might leave you in their meeting responses. You may also add each of the 26 letters of the alphabet to this list if you choose to. Click OK.

17. Click Finish. You can choose to run the rule now if you like.

Optionally, you can set up different rules for each response type and take different actions. From now on, if you've chosen to route these items to a folder, you can do a quick review of the folder contents, select them all and use Shift+Delete to permanently delete them. See Tip 19, 'Outlook: Shift+Delete', page 67.

# Tip #25

## Save Time Sending the Same Content With Quick Steps

## The Challenge

How often do you need to action different email in the same way (for example, forward an invoice to the same person and then file the original; forward the email, file it but add a reminder for yourself; add it to a page in OneNote; write an email to a specific person; create a calendar/task from an email then file it away)? It all takes time. But there is a way to automate such repetitive tasks, and especially ones needing multiple actions.

## The Solution

You can use the Quick Parts function to save time with repetitive tasks. In the Quick Steps gallery on the Home tab you will find quite a few pre-prepared actions such as (forward) To Manager, but there is so much more available with a Custom Quick Step.

Let's take a couple of specific examples to show you how Quick Parts works.

## Example 1

When you receive an invoice from a supplier, you always need to forward it to Susan in accounts and then move the original to that client's folder.

1. *Click on the down arrow* – bottom right side of the Quick Steps box and select the New dropdown menu. From this, pick Custom.

2. *Complete the Edit Quick Step dialogue as follows.* Give the new Quick Step a name. Then chose the first action by clicking on the Choose an Action down arrow. (Choose your action: there is a long list. Be patient and scroll until you find the one you want.) In this case, Forward to Susan. Then choose the next action. Move to Folder. You can keep adding actions until you have finished.

3. *Click Finish when all the actions are listed.* Then click OK.

4. Now you have a button in the Quick Step menu for this set of actions. Click on it to execute it.

## Example 2

Say you receive an email from an organisation (Decanter) which you want to glance at, move to a folder but then flag for your attention later, say the following week. Proceed as above, but here your actions are Move to Folder; Flag Message as shown below.

Now you have your own personal set of Quick Steps as shown below to use when you need.

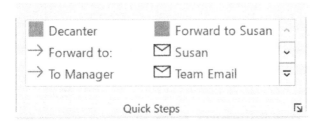

**Super user tips**

1. Change the icon in the Quick Step menu to make it easier to pick the one you want. To do this, click on the icon beside the Quick Step name and select from the icon box as shown below.

2. Re-order how the Quick Steps appear so that the ones you use most are at the top of the list. Click on the Quick Steps down arrow and use the Manage Quick Steps dialogue box. Click on the Quick Step you want to move and use the arrows beside the New button to move it up or down.

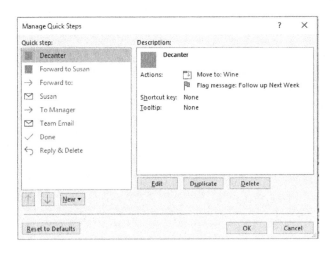

Quick Steps is a great way to automate repetitive actions, especially those which require several actions to complete like those in the examples.

# ‖ Tip #26 ‖

## Save Time Sending the Same Content With Quick Parts

### The Challenge

How often each week do you need to send the same email content but to a different person? (for example, ask for a report for the board meeting, acknowledge a CV for a job application, acknowledge receipt of an invoice or forward an invoice to accounting)?

My bet is you probably do one of the following: find the last similar email you sent and cut and paste the copy, type the reply from memory (maybe because you touch type) or copy and paste the content from a document you created in Word (or similar).

That all takes time and you can easily make errors. Did you realise you can save valuable time by using Outlook Quick Parts? Quick Parts also reduces the scope for typos, because you only have to get it right once.

# The Solution

*Quick Parts for creating 'templates' of re-usable text*

This is one of our favourite time savers, and here is how to use it to almost instantly insert the same content in an email you need to send frequently to different people.

1.  Open a new email and click in the body.

2.  Compose the text, adding any rich text or objects you need.

3.  Select it all. Then from the Insert Tab in the Text Group, click on Quick Parts. Click on Save Selection to Quick Parts Gallery at the bottom of the dropdown menu.

4.  Complete the Create New Building Block dialogue box. Give it a descriptive name so that it will be easy to recall the contents. For Quick Parts you plan to use often, use an underscore or other character in front of the name. It will appear first in the list. If you are likely to have several similar Quick Parts, you might want to add a description and use the categories to group them. To create a new category, click the Category drop down box and choose Create New Category.

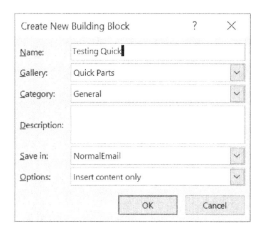

5. To use a Quick Part in a new email, place the cursor in the body of the email, click on the same Quick Parts button and select the one you wish to use.

### *How do I manage the Quick Parts Gallery to delete or edit entries?*

To delete an entry, open a new email and go to Insert an entry as in Step 5 above. Right click any entry. From the dropdown menu, select Organise and Delete. Then delete the unwanted entry.

To edit a Quick Part, insert the text into the email, then edit it and re-save it as in Steps 3 and 4 above. Give it the same name as before and confirm that you want it replaced.

---

**Pro Tip:**

To save even more time, you might want to add the Quick Parts function button to the Quick Access Tool bar. Right-click on the icon and select Add to Quick Access Toolbar.

To avoid opening the whole gallery each time, click on Insert in the body of the email and start typing the name of the specific Quick Part. As soon as the first line of the Quick Part name appears, press the Enter key.

---

# ‖ Tip #27 ‖

## Getting Feedback: Outlook Voting Buttons

## The Challenge

Getting people to respond with just the information you want can be somewhat of a challenge. If you ask them to respond to a question to which there can only be one answer, you will sometimes get that answer or a lengthy narrative about each choice and their decision-making process. How can you make it easy for them and you to get just the feedback you need?

## The Solution

One solution in Outlook is to use Voting Buttons. These work best if everyone on your recipient list is also using Outlook. Otherwise, for example in Gmail, the button to vote their choice won't be present.

### Creating a Message With Voting

Let's say you want to get lunch orders.

1. Compose your email message. It is best to include the instruction to look for the Vote button above in the ribbon.

2. Click the Use Voting Buttons button on the Options tab in the Tracking group.

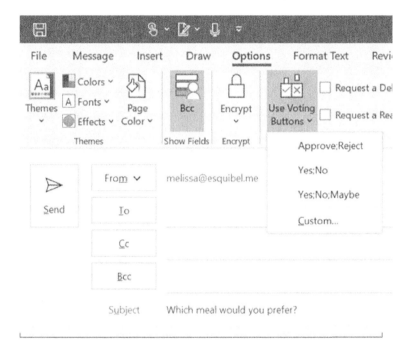

3. You can use one of the presets or, in our case, create your own list of choices by clicking Custom…

4. In the Voting and Tracking Options dialogue, the Use Voting Buttons checkbox will be checked. In the field to the right, enter your choices separated by a semi-colon (;).

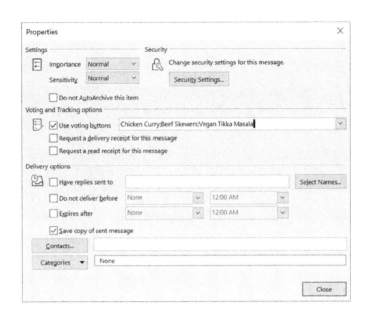

5. Click Close.

6. You will see the message confirming that you have chosen the voting option.

7. Send your message. Recipients will receive a message like this.

**Please choose one of these meals for lunch.**

## Processing Responses

This can be a bit irregular depending upon how the message comes back to you. Optimally, you would locate your sent message in the Sent folder and click the Tracking button to see what has come back to you. However, you may just see the responses coming back with the response in the subject line, like this:

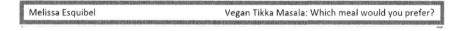

Another way they could come back to you is with the response in the notifications section of the reply email.

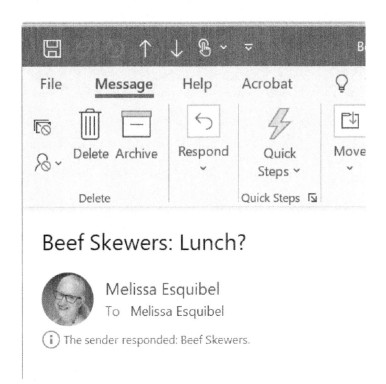

The inconsistency makes this a good option for internal usage where the responders are all using Outlook within your organisation. Once you know how these will come back to you, it will be easy to know how to process the feedback. Should your field of respondents be wider, it might be best to use either Microsoft Forms or Google Forms (see Tip 96, 'Getting Feedback: Google Forms', page 355, and Tip 97, 'Getting Feedback: Microsoft Forms', page 361).

# | Tip #28 |

## Performing a Mail Merge in Outlook

## The Challenge

Are you still using the bcc: line to send the same message to multiple people? There are many good reasons not to do that. First, some spam filters will bounce your message to the trash if it has too many addressees and they don't care where they are in the message header! Second, it may look a bit amateurish. Third, there's no way to really personalise the message for multiple people. So, what do you do instead? You could work with an email management program like Constant Contact or MailChimp. Or, you could just use native Outlook!

## The Solution

Did you know that you could perform a mail merge directly in Microsoft Outlook? You will actually be performing the fundamental steps of the merge in Word, but you will begin in Outlook in People/Contacts.

1. First, identify the contacts (not contact groups) to whom you would like to send a merged message. I recommend using a List view or any view that allows you to select contacts and see clearly

who you've selected. Alternatively, you can create a temporary folder and copy these contacts into that folder. That way there's no chance you will actually send it to your whole contact list, if you didn't mean to. (Yikes!)

2.  Next, on the Home tab, in the Actions group, click the Mail Merge button. This will bring you to this dialogue box.

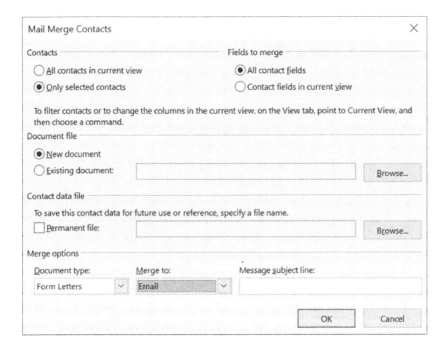

3.  The «Only selected contacts» radio button will be selected by default. Don't change it. Leave all other settings in place as well, changing only the 'Merge to' field to Email. Enter a message subject line in the field provided.

4.  Click OK. You will be taken to Word and the Mailings tab. From here you will use the Write & Insert Fields group buttons to create your message.

5.  Now, before moving on from here, return to Outlook. On the Send/Receive tab, click the Work Offline button on the far right. When you complete your merge in the next steps, it will

automatically place all your messages in the outbox. This gives you one more opportunity to see who will get messages and what they look like before setting them free to go to their intended recipients. It's really handy for recognizing that you've accidentally sent it to 100 people when you intended a mailing list of only 10!

6. Click on Preview Results and arrow though them to make sure they look correct.

7. Finally, click Finish & Merge in the Finish group and choose to Send Email. Here you can adjust the subject line or select records to include. The merged messages will now appear as individual messages in the Outbox. If you should open any to review, be sure to click on Send to close it. Otherwise, it may not go out. Once you're satisfied with your messages, turn Work Offline off. And off they'll go!

# | Tip #29 |

## Outlook Mobile: What Can It Do?

## The Challenge

As much as Microsoft endeavours to make its various versions of Outlook which are intended to function on different devices as similar as possible, the differences exist. And, for the administrative professional, it can limit what you are able to do using your smaller devices, whether Android or iOS. A secondary challenge many administrative professionals face is that they are provided with only Outlook Online rather than the desktop version of Outlook. This is tantamount to handing a surgeon a butter knife when what they really need is a scalpel. Most information workers do not use Outlook as deeply as administrative professionals use them.

## The Solution

### Things that work across devices

The first step is to understand what is the same across all the device versions. This helps set an expectation of what you will be able to do from a remote device. Here is a list of features that fit that description (as of November 2020).

- Compose New Message/Reply
  - Attach files
  - Attach links to files from OneDrive for Business
  - Insert/change signatures

- Connect to other accounts
  - Exchange Server
  - Microsoft 365 Exchange Online

- Contacts
  - Exchange Server
  - Microsoft 365 Exchange Online

- Mailbox controls
  - Print
  - Set automatic replies (Out of Office)
  - Work Offline

- Mail-Folder pane
  - Clutter folder
  - Create new folder
  - Folders list
  - Microsoft 365 Groups

- Message list actions
  - Conversation view
  - Flag/Follow up
  - Focused Inbox
  - Move to Spam folder
  - Use conversation view or classic

- Search
  - Local search
  - Server search

## Things that don't work on the Outlook iOS app

The following actions cannot be done on the Outlook app for iOS.

- Compose New Message/Reply
  - Add Voting buttons
  - Alias support Outlook.com
  - Follow Up/Flag when creating email
  - MailTips – for example, recipient is out of office
  - Set High/Low importance

- Mailbox controls
  - Create inbox rules

- Mail-Folder pane
  - Access to Public Folders
  - Favourite folders list
  - Rename folder
  - View PSTs
  - View/Send mail from Shared Mailboxes

- Message list actions
  - Assign archive or retention policies
  - Categorize
  - Clean up thread
  - Empty Spam folder
  - Ignore conversation
  - Mark as Clutter
  - Report as junk

## Things that don't work on the Android app

The following actions cannot be done on the Outlook app for Android.

- Compose New Message/Reply
    - Add Voting buttons
    - Alias support Outlook.com
    - Attach links to files from OneDrive for Business
    - Follow Up/Flag when creating email
    - MailTips - for example, recipient is out of office
    - Set High/Low importance

- Mailbox controls
    - Create inbox rules

- Mail-Folder pane
    - Access to Public Folders
    - Favourite folders list
    - Rename folder
    - View PSTs
    - View/Send mail from Shared Mailboxes

- Message list actions
    - Assign archive or retention policies
    - Categorize
    - Clean up thread
    - Empty Spam folder
    - Ignore conversation
    - Mark as Clutter
    - Report as junk

## What to Do About It

The case for having the Outlook app compatible with your device is that you can do the most basic of functions, such as creating, checking and replying to email, making new folders and moving email to them. Remember that any inbox rules you've created that run on Exchange will still run, regardless of what device you see the messages on. You won't be able to create new ones, but they will operate just the same. Microsoft does keep adding functionality to the mobile apps, so the above information may change from time to time.

The bottom line is that the mobile versions of Microsoft Outlook are not robust enough to be used as the primary device for the normal responsibilities an administrative professional would need in order to provide an appropriate level of support. If you are asked to use the online version (web version) of Outlook, you will need additional training. While most of the functionality in the desktop app is there, it is often not where you expect it to be!

And, finally, using any version of Outlook that does not allow you to access important information regardless of your internet connection leaves you and your organisation vulnerable to not being able to react in urgent situations.

# ‖ **Tip #30** ‖

## Creating Templates in Outlook

## The Challenge

Have you ever copied a previous email message because it contains all of the things you want to say in a new one, then forgotten to change the salutation? It's a bit awkward for Richard to read an email addressed 'Dear Samantha'. There are several techniques you can use to avoid that embarrassment. One of them is to create a template.

## The Solution

Quick Steps are great for creating a text only email or reply, but they do not allow rich text (bold, italic, coloured fonts), hyperlinks, graphics or attachments. Using one or more Quick Parts is fine to add to a new message, too. However, you can create a complete email template which contains everything you need and use it to create a new message or direct a reply using the template from a rule.

Here are the steps to create a template

1. Create a new message.
2. Type all of your text attach any attachments which are static (won't change from message to message). Erase any signature that automatically appears.

Your signature will be added when you create a message using this template.

3. You can also add any email addresses at the top that will not change (for example, addresses in the cc: line).
4. Click the File tab, then Save As, then More options…
5. Change the 'Save as type' field to Outlook Template.
6. Name your template and click Save.
7. Close the message you are composing and choose not to save it. (Don't worry, it's saved as a template!)

To use your template

1. On the Home tab in the New group, click the New Items button and select More Items, then Choose Form.
2. Change the 'Look in' field to User Templates in File System.
3. Locate and select your template. Click Open.

You'll notice your standard signature for new messages at the bottom you can change this to an alternative signature if you wish. You can also change anything else you wish about the message before sending.

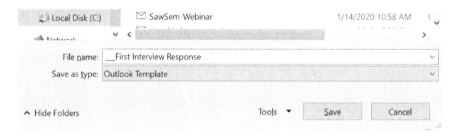

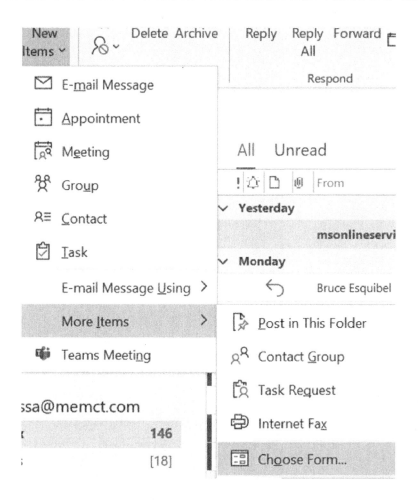

To activate a template in a rule, in the 'Step 1: What do you want to do with the message' dialogue, locate and check the box next to Reply using a specific template. Then click the link to locate your template in User Templates in File System.

# Tip #31

## Dictation: Let Your Voice Do the Typing in Outlook

## The Challenge

Whether your motivation to avoid typing on a keyboard is technical, medical or simply that your keyboarding skills are not awesome, using the Dictate function in Microsoft Outlook can enable you to take advantage of this alternative to typing text. The Dictate function is present as well in Word and PowerPoint. This function is already included in the native installation of Microsoft 365 and is available for Office 2016, so there's nothing additional to install. On a Mac, you'll need to be running Office for Mac 16.40 (20042602) or later.

## The Solution

To compose an email message with your voice, do the following.

- Click the Compose button to begin a new email message.
- Click on the Dictate button in the Voice group on the right side of the ribbon.
- Just start speaking. You will see the text appear.

You can use this feature in the address fields; however, the results may be inconsistent. To ensure you send the right message to the right people, you might want to type these yourself. Once you have clicked into the body of the message, you can pretty much just talk. Say words like 'period' or 'full stop' to get it to type a period. You can also say the words 'new line' to get it to make a new paragraph. If you navigate away from the email window, it will turn the Dictate function off. You will need to re-enable it by clicking it.

> **Pro Tip:**
>
> Add the Dictate button to the Quick Access Toolbar to make your own shortcut with the Alt key!

At first, it may not use the exact words you are speaking, but eventually it learns what you mean when you say certain things. It may not get punctuation or capitalisation correct. You will likely need to proofread and edit, with a little more editing than you might be used to. However, you will not have had to type the whole message. For slow typists, this is a timesaver. For fast typists, it may seem like a bit more trouble to begin with, but eventually sore wrists and shoulders may thank you!

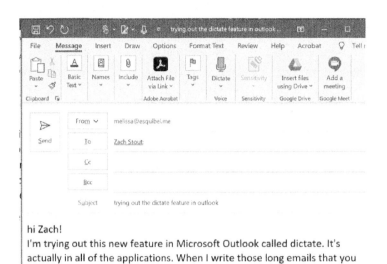

hi Zach!
I'm trying out this new feature in Microsoft Outlook called dictate. It's actually in all of the applications. When I write those long emails that you love so much I don't have to Thai up my wrist or hands

## Monica's Journey in Switching from Keyboard to Voice Typing

I resorted to trying dictation when my osteoarthritis (OA) flared up in protest at the combination of typing a book, gardening and playing golf. The dictation function was a great help for email. A little patience was needed in the beginning, but it very quickly learned my voice and certain words. Changing behaviour from typing to dictation took a few goes too. I'd find myself starting to type before remembering to switch on Dictation.

The only annoying part is that if you stop typing and switch to a different screen, the dictation stops and you need to remember to reactivate it.

Certainly, for email it was a great help. Working on documents and presentations was harder for me personally, but that is more a reflection of how I work. Dictation is a skill at which some are very good, such as doctors and senior government officials, and is worth learning for anyone suffering long-term OA related conditions.

Did it save time and help me improve my productivity? Time, no, but if you regard wellbeing as a key factor to being productive, yes.

# Tip #32

## Dictation: Let Your Voice Do the Typing in Gmail

## The Challenge

Whether your motivation to avoid typing on a keyboard is technical, medical or simply that your keyboarding skills are not awesome, using the Chrome extension Dictation for Gmail can enable you to take advantage of this alternative to typing text.

## The Solution

### Preparation

First, make sure your computer's microphone is working. Next, you will need to add the Dictation for Gmail Chrome extension.

- From Google search, locate the Chrome Web Store and choose the result for Extensions.

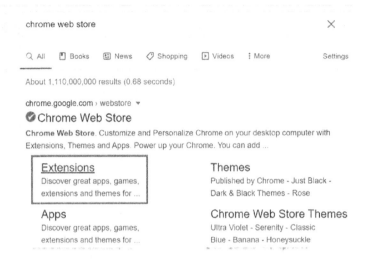

- Next, in the Search in store field, type 'gmail dictation'. You will see the extension show up in the search results.

- Click the entry to see the Add to Chrome button. Click it. Confirm that you want to add the extension.

- Close the tab once it confirms that it has been added. You will need to close any compose window you have open in Gmail and refresh the Gmail screen to begin using the tool.

## Using Dictation for Gmail

Now you're ready to start composing email with your voice.

1. Click the Compose button to begin a new email message.

2. You will now see a little microphone at the bottom of the compose window in the toolbar.

3. The first time you click it, it will ask permission to use your microphone. Allow it.

4. Click into the body of the email and just start speaking. You will see the text appear.

At first, it may not use the exact words you are speaking, but eventually it learns what you mean when you say certain things. It may not get punctuation or capitalisation correct. You will likely need to proofread and edit, with a little more editing than you might be used to. However, you will not have had to type the whole message. For slow typists, this is a timesaver. For fast typists, it may seem like a bit more trouble to begin with, but eventually sore wrists and shoulders may thank you!

Recipients

Subject

This is an email being dictated with my voice. this was done by adding the dictation for Gmail Chrome extension.

You may need to go back and edit the message you recorded because so words may not be interpreted correctly. overtime the system will learn how speak and what words you commonly use, such as

I was saying Chrome the entire time, but it interpreted it as Crown, from, a Chrome.
crown from chrome chrome chrome Chrome

Send   EN ▾  A  ⊖ ☺  !

# | Tip #33 |

## See Email Messages as They Arrive Only From Key People

### The Challenge

We all know that the most productive people stay focused on the task at hand, be it talking to someone or booking a flight. That means turning off all those new email messages and social media notifications.

Ah, but we hear the cry, 'What if the boss/key client email messages me with an urgent request (for example, the boss with urgent changes to their travel plans, a meeting, a key client wanting to update an order)?'

### The Solution

1. Agree on one particular medium for urgent matters, for example the phone or WhatsApp.

2. If email is the preferred channel, write a rule which prompts you when email messages arrive from this key person. That prompt could be a box with the highlights of the email or a sound. Here is how you do it.

   a) Right-click on the person's name. From the dropdown menu, select Create Rule.

b) From the Rules Wizard, click on Advanced Options.

c) From the Step 1 box, click on the box with the person's name.

d) Click Next

e) In the next box, click on the relevant action - for example, Display a Desktop Alert. Click Next/Next/Finish.

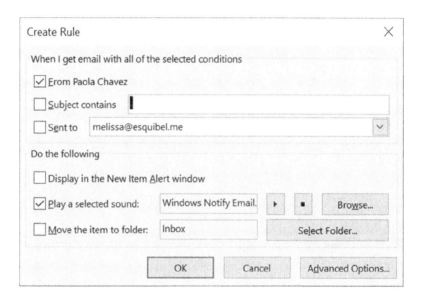

You can have a sound as the alert, though it might not be wise if you are in an open-plan office. But if you do choose the sound option at stage (e), you will need to select a sound by clicking Browse or accept the default sound indicated. Press the Play button to hear it.

Now you can stay focused in the secure knowledge that you will never miss an email from a key contact, but you will not need to be distracted by all the other email messages which can wait until you choose to stop what you are doing and look at the inbox.

# | Tip #34 |

## Handle Each Email Message Only Once – The Four Ds Principle

### The Challenge

After a while, email messages pile up in my inbox, and on a bad day I can have 300+ items in there. Then I spend time scrolling through checking and re-checking email messages to make sure I've not missed anything.

Is there a way to reduce this time spent scrolling up and down the inbox without using up precious time for filing?

### The Solution

Yes. The key to improving your productivity is to treat your inbox as 'work in-hand' and thus make sure you action each email as you open (read) it. Adopt the four Ds principle of time management, and for Outlook users, consider using the Conversation View and Quick Steps functions. (See 'Quick Steps to Save Time and Deal with Email'.)

### The Four Ds Principle

First and foremost, never just flip through your inbox randomly. Always try to triage it, sorting by person, subject, date, etc., whatever suits you best. If there are several from the same person on the same topic, make sure you have the Conversation view on (go to the View tab and click on Show as Conversations) as shown below. Messages which form a conversation are now marked with a little triangle beside them.

Now, and this is the critical time-saver, action the message by doing one of these four Ds.

- *DEAL with it* – Respond here and now (be that to read or respond to it). Your folder structure can be complex or simple. Neither is better or worse. The critical point is to move the email out of the inbox once you have actioned it. We look at folders in more detail in To Folder or Not

- *DELETE it* – It's old and past its sell-by date and of no real value either to you or your business.

- *DELEGATE* – Pass it to someone to either action on your behalf or prepare a response for you.

- *DEFER* – You cannot deal with it now but it does need action. Tell the recipient when it will be actioned and add a reminder for yourself. See 'Insert a Reminder in Recipient's Email', page 217.

In this way you should quickly be able to keep your inbox under control and save yourself time. Furthermore, the very act of moving email messages you have dealt with to a separate folder acts as an emotional sign of achievement.

## OK, but what about the backlog of email messages already in my inbox?

Easy! Move all the old messages out to a specific new folder which you can sort through later. Start the new folder with either a full stop "." Or a hyphen "-" and it will sit at the top of your folder list for easy access. Alternatively, move it to your Favourites list for easy access.

What constitutes old is a personal choice, but we would suggest anything over three weeks. If you have not actioned an item that old, either it's out of date (and perhaps irrelevant) or the sender will have re-emailed you as a reminder!

# | Tip #35 |

## Audit Your Inbox to Find the Root Cause of Cc'd Email Messages

*If I'm sending email messages, and I get all wound up and stressed and don't know what to do with myself for 20 minutes, I just go soak in hot water and lie there, thinking, 'What should I do?' So, it's meditative.*
*— Tom Ford*

### The Challenge

Whenever we ask EAs and PAs 'What is the main challenge you face dealing with your inbox?', top of the list is all the cc'd email messages. Often there is a rider 'Not only my own inbox but also in my executive's inbox. We often both receive the same message when only one of us really needs it. How can we reduce the number of cc'd email messages?'

### The Solution

One of us has sat in Tom Ford's office but not his bath! Meditating will not reduce the volume of cc'd email messages, but auditing your (and your executive's) inbox will help identify the underlying cause.

## Audit the Inbox

Take a typical few days' email messages and proceed as follows:

- Count the number.

- Cluster/group the messages by sender.

- Identify potential patterns - for example, which of the reasons in the next section fits the sender's email message behaviour.

The underlying cause of so many cc'd email messages is a lack of clear understanding about who needs what information and what information is of real relevance to the recipient (either you or your executive).

## Common Causes of Cc'd Email Messages and Action to Take

The common potential causes and appropriate actions you can take to reduce cc'd messages are as follows. In most instances, the key action is to communicate politely to the sender what you do and do not need.

| | Potential cause of the cc'd email messages | Action to reduce the cc'd email messages |
|---|---|---|
| | The sender's perception is that they | |
| 1 | Think you might be interested in the content. | Communicate what you do and do not need/are interested in. |
| 2 | Does not know who really needs the message; you or your executive. | Agree with your executive who needs what information and then communicate this to the sender(s) |
| 3 | Is worried about missing out a key person, so they add everyone who might be interested. | Communicate what you do and do not need/are interested in. |
| 4 | Cover their backside: 'I told you, so I am in the clear if this becomes a problem'. | Explain that this is not a very healthy organisation culture and that such messages waste everyone's time. |
| 5 | Playing the self-promotion game by telling everyone what they are doing and how busy they have been. | Suggest they stop behaving in this way. Remind them that actions speak louder than words. If they are truly performing well then, they will be noticed. |
| 6 | Needs positive feedback and strokes as they are feeling insecure/worried. In times of stress and uncertainty like the COVID pandemic, studies have found that the volume of email traffic rises considerably. | Give verbal positive feedback and suggest they stop sending so many cc'd email messages. |
| 7 | Playing politics; by adding your executive to the cc line, they either feel they may gain their attention or are trying to work around you (for some questionable reason). | Ask them face-to-face what is going on and what are they hoping to achieve. |
| 8 | Believes that you/your boss want to know what they are doing. | Discuss with your executive who needs what information and then communicate this to the sender(s). |
| | In addition, | |
| 9 | Your executive is a micro manager and has asked all their team to cc them regardless | There is not much you can do other than help your executive to stop micromanaging! |
| 10 | You are on a distribution list to which you probably did not subscribe. | Either remove yourself or write a rule to send these specific email messages to a folder outside your inbox. See Tips 12a and 12b. |

Try to start with 'Thank you, however I/we are trying to save time dealing with email messages to improve my/our productivity/ performance/wellbeing. Please can you help by...'

**Pro Tip:**

As you will realise, in some instances this is a change in behaviour/culture. Therefore, you may have to repeat the directive many times because people often do not believe you the first time. You will also need to demonstrate the desired behaviour yourself to help senders change their behaviour and attitude.

# Tip #36

## Email Management Apps

## The Challenge

I've heard colleagues talk about apps which can help you manage your inbox by, for example, reminding you about email messages which need your attention. What are these apps, how do they work and what are the best ones?

## The Solution

There are basically three types of email management apps, those which:

1. Use artificial intelligence (AI) to learn which email you regard as important and filter your incoming email accordingly.
2. Can be used to send away email which you do not wish to deal with at present and bring them back to your inbox when you are ready (you have given the return date).
3. Suggest how you might reply to certain email messages by presenting you with pre-prepared templates of text, emoticons, etc.

Two important points to note: First, some apps are specific to certain email platforms such as Gmail. Second, if you work in a large corporate environment you may not be allowed to use them on your business email account.

Therefore, these email management apps are often best suited to Virtual PAs and those EAs and PAs working in entrepreneurial-type organisations.

There are many such apps, and new ones appear almost as often as do new email messages. Here are a few of the more well-established, tried and tested apps.

## Apps Which Filter Email Based on AI

**SaneBox** – This learns what is important to you and moves all the nonimportant email into a folder for you to read later. It works with most common email platforms (Gmail, Outlook, Mail), but does not support POP based accounts.

**Knowmail** – Like Sanebox it learns via AI what is important to you, and helps prioritise which email messages you see and in addition how you might respond.

**Edison** – This is more like a complete email platform. It allows you to batch email, unsubscribe and send email messages away until you are ready to deal with them. It works with Apple Mail, Gmail and Microsoft Outlook Windows version.

**Unroll.me** – This just deals with all the newsletters and promotional email messages that you don't want to clutter up your inbox but at the same time don't want to unsubscribe from. It scans your inbox, learns and allows you to unsubscribe en masse, or it batches such email up into one daily briefing email with headlines from each newsletter, etc.

## Apps Which Remind You When to Action Email

**Nudgemail** – No need to resend yourself an email. Instead, send it to your Nudgemail account and it re-appears in your inbox on a future date specified by you. Works on all platforms.

Boomerang – Specifically for Gmail users. It not only lets you send away email messages you don't want to deal with at present but also lets you write email messages to be sent at a future date (e.g., reminders to colleagues when you are away from work). Both Nudge mail and Boomerang mean more email in your inbox as the reminders fly back in.

*Inbox Ready* – This basically hides your inbox, leaving you distraction-free to deal with other email-related tasks such as sending new email messages and managing your calendar and task list. One click and your inbox re-appears.

*Dispatch* – A dedicated iPhone app. This lets you archive email messages to Evernote and Pocket to read later, but it does not support POP accounts.

## Apps Which Provide Pre-Prepared Reply Text

These are generally designed to help marketers improve their open rates. Nonetheless, five struck us as useful.

*Canned Email* – A website with templates of text for a variety of situations (for example, having sick leave, just needing to say thank you, acknowledging an email asking you to do something, etc.).

*FoxType* – a Chrome extension which takes what you write and offers different versions which may sound more friendly or more assertive.

*The Readability Checker* – A website which rates how easy the content of your message is to read/understand. Useful if you are working in a global environment where not everyone's mother tongue is English. (It currently only supports English.)

*Hemingway* – Very similar to the Readability Checker, but it offers alternative wording.

*EmailAnalytics* – This is in a category of its own. Basically, it audits the email traffic through your inbox and tells you how many email messages you send and receive, when, and who your main senders and recipients are. Using the data, you can build up a picture of your communications paths and identify where to spend more or less time and how to improve the use of your time.

## Pros and Cons of Email Management Apps

The major email platforms all have facilities which can perform most of these functions - for example, rules for filtering, Quick Parts (in Outlook for creating templates) and flags for reminding you when to action an email. It is about exploring what you already have and learning to use the relevant facilities.

Of the aforementioned apps, those which do stand out as offering something different and which we know many EAs and PAs use are Unroll.me, Inbox Ready, Sanebox and EmailAnalytics. Most offer free trials which allow you to evaluate the benefits (or not) to yourself.

# Tip #37

## To Folder or Not

### The Challenge

Some people have very complex folder structures with multiple folders. Others have simple ones with very few folders. Which is best?

### The Solution

First and foremost, you need to see the email in your inbox as the work in hand which needs your attention, be they new or old email. This means moving email out of the inbox once you have actioned them using the 4Ds process – See 'Handle Each Email Message Only Once - The Four Ds Principle'.

Thus, you need some type of folder structure; how complex is a matter of personal preference. Whichever folder structure you use, remember not to let the filing become a task which eats up too much time.

## Complex Folder Structures – Four Tips to Save Time

- Create folders which are logical, such as by project, person, client or event.

- Avoid creating a folder for every new project/event. Where you only have a few email messages in a sub-folder, consider amalgamating them into one.

- If you cannot decide where to put an item, this indicates that your folder structure is too complex.

- If there are two logical places for an email message, you can make a copy of the email and place it in two places or use a search folder based on some criteria in the message for the second one. If you absolutely must save an email in two different folders:

  o File the email in the first folder.

  o Select it again and with the right mouse button held down, drag it to the other folder.

  o From the dropdown menu, select Copy.

## Simple Folder Structures – Four Top Tips

- Keep the structure really simple. Imagine your folders are a big dustbin.

- Limit the total number of folders to no more than 10 (otherwise you are moving towards the complex end).

- Make the labels meaningful to you.

- A typical simple five folder structure could be:

  o Completed. All email you want to keep and which have been fully actioned.

  o Ditch/Archived. Unless you truly want to delete an email, don't just put it in the Trash folder because some systems are set to empty the Trash folder at set intervals. Then you run the risk of losing an old email to which you really might want to refer back. Instead, create a dedicated folder for such email.

  o Delegated – awaiting a response. Good practice suggests adding a reminder flag.

o   Ideas – as the name suggests, possible contacts to
     followup, news items of current interest, etc.

o   Events – tickets, travel details, etc.

## Complex or Simple Folder Structure – Five Golden Rules

1.  Some advocate having a specific folder for email you need to
    action later. But that means you must check the folder regularly.
    Instead, adopt a robust reminder process.
2.  Remember that folders should be seen as a means to an end,
    namely a way of helping you keep a clean inbox and hence not
    the end itself.
3.  The 'clean inbox' concept is a better use of your time than
    spending too much time trying to reach inbox zero.
4.  Make sure you review the folders regularly to ensure you are
    not keeping email which is in breach of the GDPR.
5.  Evaluate the overall structure from time to time because your
    priorities will change as might your email software.

For tips on organisation in Gmail, see Using labels and stars in Gmail.

# ‖ Tip #38 ‖

## Don't Make Copies of Email Messages, Use Search Folders Instead

## The Challenge

Making copies of email messages exacerbates a problem you probably already have: too much email. However, that technique is generally applied when a message applies to more than one project or a project *and* a person. Back when the search function in Outlook was not as robust as it is today, this method didn't seem like such a bad idea. However, there is an easier, less bulky way to manage the challenge of filing an email message in more than one place.

## The Solution

Search Folders can be used in ways you may not have considered. You already have one out-of-the-box called Unread. One very useful Search Folder can be called 'Today' that just looks at items received today, whether read or unread. On a day where you can't stem the tide of email messages flooding into your inbox, you can always go to Today or Unread to get the new things right in front of you. You can also set up Search Folders for your VIPs whose messages you must respond to quickly. Show them all in Favourites to stay on top of what's important.

Search Folders aren't actually 'folders'. They are really just a saved search. Outlook items remain wherever you have them and will also appear in whatever Search Folder for which the search criteria applies. Just like that, no more copies!

## To Set Up a Search Folder

1. Locate the Search Folders listing in your Navigation Pane. It appears below the Outbox on each account you have.

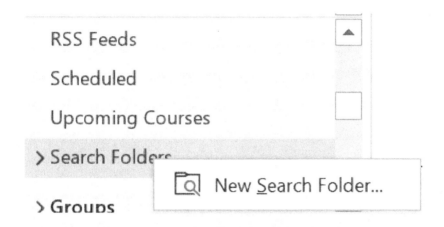

2. Right-click it and choose New Search Folder.

3. Select one of the ones listed or choose 'Create a custom Search Folder'.

4. For more criteria choices click the 'Criteria…' button.

5. Specify your criteria and click OK.

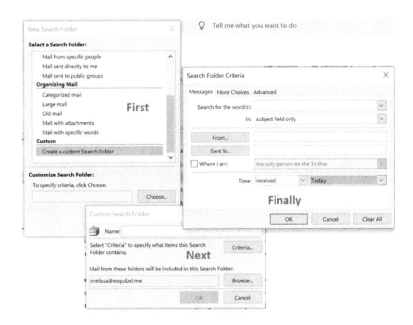

6.  Right click your new Search Folder and select Add to Favourites

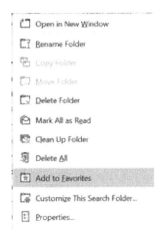

# Tip #39

## Editing an Email to Show the Action Taken

### The Challenge

With a shared inbox (for example, boss and EA, sales@), can you annotate an email to show if you have taken action (for example, replied, forwarded it for more information)? This can be so useful when one of us wants to add a comment and leave the original email in the main inbox.

### The Solution

Yes, the function is found in different places in Outlook for Windows and Outlook for Mac. As of this writing, it is not possible to do this in Gmail.

### Outlook for Windows

1. Open the message.

2. From the Move group on the Message tab, click on the Actions button (or More Move Actions, depending upon the version) and choose Edit message.

3. Make your changes.

4. Close the message and click Save when you are prompted to save changes.

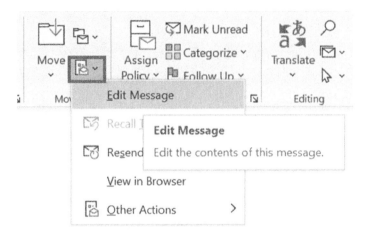

## Outlook for Mac

1. Open the message.

2. From the Message menu, select Edit message.

3. Make your changes.

4. Close and select the Save option.

NOTE: On a Mac you can also edit the message from the preview pane.

---

**Pro Tip:**

If you are accessing the inbox with full administration rights, why not add a Category to edited messages to catch the other person's eye? This can make it easy for them to see where an email has such extra information.

---

# ‖ Tip #40 ‖

## When to Use a Read Receipt

When you ask a group of administrative professionals: 'What does a Read Receipt accomplish in Outlook or Gmail?', many will answer: 'Well, it tells you that they've read it!'

## The Challenge

That may have been the original intention of this feature, but it is not what it actually does, technically speaking. Technically, when the Unread flag is switched off by opening an email, if a Read Receipt has been requested, a prompt is delivered to the reader to ask if the receipt should be sent to the message sender.

Did you spot the two problems? First, all the reader did was open the email. We really don't have any idea if they read it. Secondly, they would actually have to opt to send you that receipt. Spammers have figured out this neat feature, too! They use it to determine whether they have a valid email address.

More bad news: I can switch the Uunread flag off in a rule based on some criteria, like sender or subject. Never opened it, and might never see it in the list either because I can also set up the rule to move it to a folder.

## The Solution

Like many priority-inferring features, Read Receipts can be useful if you decide, ahead of time with your teams and work groups, what they mean. For example, on my work teams, a Read Receipt means that the recipient is responsible for knowing this information and conducting business based on this information from close of business of the sent date. It is only used internally on our work teams.

The only other reason to use a Read Receipt is part of a technical test along with a Delivery Receipt when you're trying to determine whether email servers are behaving properly. You would of course communicate in advance to your intended message reader what you are doing and that you need the Read Receipt returned. Unless you're a spammer.

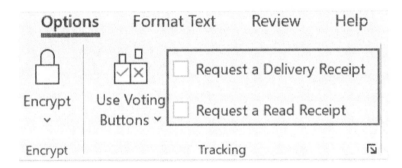

# | Tip #41 |

## Recalling Messages: The Hard Truth

### The Challenge

You hit send. And, even as your finger is letting off the Enter key, something in your brain is screaming, 'Nooooooo!!!' The hard truth about recalling email messages is that, just like the wrong words, once they've left your mouth, they can't effectively be 'recalled.' Here is what is meant by 'effectively.'

In Outlook, a recall will only work if the message remains unread and in the recipient's inbox, and really only if they're in your organisation with their email being processed on the same Exchange Server. If they have written a rule to set the Unread flag off or move it to another folder, a recall is an 'information only' message. Many can't resist being told that they are not supposed to read something that is right there, able to be read. So, saying you didn't mean to send it potentially only has the effect of exclaiming, 'Oops!' after making a mistake.

In Gmail, you actually do have a few seconds in which the act of sending an email can be undone. After that, you're in the same boat as Outlook users. While you can extend the time from 5 to 30 seconds in settings, you still have to be pretty quick to realise your error.

# The Solution

There are a few things you can do to give yourself a chance against the inevitability of sending something in error.

## Outlook

### *Delay Delivery*

If you have the presence of mind to realise that the email may have some unintended consequences, but really want to send it, you can choose Delay Delivery. While composing a message, click the Options tab and the Delay Delivery button. You can specify the time to release it from the Outbox. Until that time you can delete it from the Outbox and no one will be the wiser.

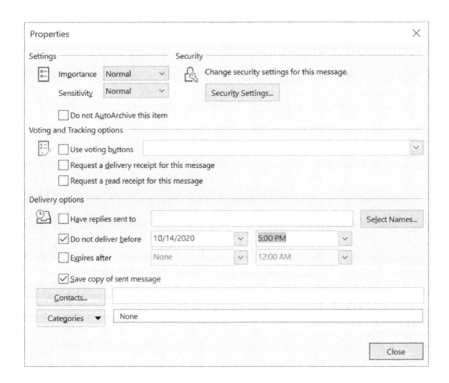

Mac users – The Delay Send is found by opening the dropdown menu (chevron) beside the Send button. A pop up window appears as shown below.

## Quick Steps

Instead of using the send button, you can set up a Quick Step which automatically delays delivery. You do have to get into the habit of hitting the Quick Step instead of Send. Set up a 'New E-mail To...' Quick Step. Then, click the checkbox next to 'Automatically send after 1 minute delay.' Naming it 'Send Message' might help with adopting this new habit.

## Rule

Set up a rule that automatically delays the send action.

1. In the Ribbon on the Home tab, click the Rules button in the Move group.

2. Choose Manage Rules and Alerts, then New Rule.

3. In the 'Start from a blank rules section,' choose 'Apply rule on messages I send.' Leave the first dialogue as is and click Next.

4. You will be presented with a dialogue asking you to confirm that you want it to apply to all messages that you send. Click Yes.

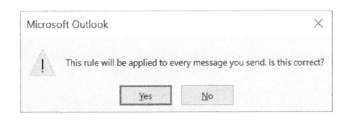

5. Check the box to the left of 'defer delivery by a number of minutes'.

6. Click the words 'a number of' in the Step 2 box at the bottom of the dialogue.

7. Enter the number of minutes you want to delay sending.

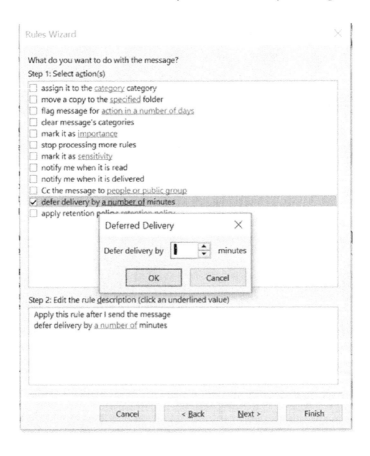

## Gmail

As mentioned above, you can undo sending a message. Initially, if you're quick enough, you can click Cancel on the Send action. After that, you can click on Undo in the lower left corner when it pops up. This puts your message back in edit mode, where you can reconsider your message.

You can change the time it will delay sending by clicking the Settings gear in the upper right corner, then 'See all settings'. In the Undo Send section, change the number of seconds to delay.

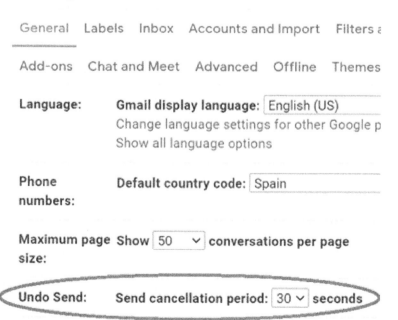

## Any Email Application

The best time to recall a message is before you send it. Read, proofread, reread and ruminate before sending. Technology behaves unexpectedly from time to time and so do we, 30 seconds or 1 minute is often not enough time to reconsider sending an email. See 'Top Tips to Avoid an Email Disaster' for more information.

# Tip #42

## Avoid Email Disaster When Forwarding an Email

## The Challenge

A colleague told me that someone had forwarded an email to her regarding a client enquiry. The email had been forwarded to several people over time and the complaint was still unresolved. As she scrolled through the email to understand the problem, she found one of the previous people had made some very unpleasant comments about her! Not surprisingly, she has now lodged a formal complaint with the HR Department about the comments. The resolution will now cost precious time and money. How could this unpleasant situation have been avoided?

## The Solution

Here are seven guidelines to which you should always adhere when forwarding an email to reduce the risk of a breach of security and confidentiality and hence a possible 'emailgate' disaster like this one.

1. Always scroll through the entire email and edit out any content (entries) which might cause embarrassment to the new

recipient. For more information about editing an email message see Editing an Email to Show Action Taken.

2. In Microsoft Outlook, open the email message, go to the Move tab and select More Move Actions, then Edit Message.

   - On a Mac, from the Message menu pick Edit.

3. Always tell the other person why you are forwarding the email to them and if appropriate what action you expect them to take.

4. Alternatively (and possibly as well), use the subject line to indicate why you are forwarding the email and what action is needed and by when. Using abbreviations such as FYI or; NRN (no response needed) can help save time.

5. Think before hitting send and ask yourself what value you are adding to the recipient by forwarding the email. It is easy to hit 'forward' because you feel an email might be of interest. Don't be the one who clutters up other people's inboxes with unnecessary email. Take a few minutes to ask the other person if such messages are of interest to them. That way you are not only demonstrating excellent email behaviour, but you might also make a new friend.

6. Check that the original email is genuine, especially if the email contains breaking news. These are just the sort of subject lines that hackers use for email which either contain malware or are phishing. For more information about this, see Spot the Fake Email.

7. Respect others' privacy. Avoid forwarding email which contain gossip, personal information or comments which should not be circulated.

8. Delete contact information from the original message, as this could fall into the wrong hands and/or constitute a breach of confidentiality, security and the General Data Protection Regulation (GDPR).

# Tip #43

## Drag and Drop Email to Tasks, Calendar or People

### The Challenge

Copy and paste is nice, but there is a fast way to create one type of Outlook item from another, (for example, creating a new contact from an email, an email from a calendar item, a task from a calendar item or email).

### The Solution

Copy and paste? Meet drag and drop! Whether you use Compact Navigation or not (see examples below), you can drag an item from one menu to another. The item doesn't actually move, per se. A copy of the item is made in the format of the other item.

Here are various ways to employ this timesaving tip.

- Create a task from an email by dragging it to Tasks. You may delete the email message from your inbox, if you choose.

- Drag an email message to People (Contacts). Outlook will prefill the contact with several fields from the email message and put the rest of the email message in comments. This can be useful if you are tracking how the person first became a contact. Sales-people find this one particularly useful! You can also then drag and drop data from the comment section into the fields of the Contact form, if they have included information like company names, titles or, phone numbers.

- Drag a calendar item to Mail to create a message to someone who needs to be aware of a meeting, but perhaps not attend - for example, if someone will be filling in for you to set up the meeting room, needs to order lunch or must set up the videoconferencing portal.

- Drag a calendar item to Tasks to put setting up the meeting room, ordering food and preparing any meeting materials on your to-do list.

- Drag an email message to Calendar to create a meeting from the text of the message. It will not necessarily fill all the 'To' line people into the invitation list like the Reply with Meeting button, but it will allow you to change it from an appointment to a meeting easily by inviting people.

---

**Pro Tip:**

Perhaps not EVERYTHING in the email message needs to make it into the invitation text. Edit out anything that might be questionable. For an example, see the table on the next page.

---

| Email Text | Edited Meeting Text |
|---|---|
| I'm tired of chasing these guys, so I've set up a meeting so we can discuss the following:<br><br>1. When is the new projected completion date?<br><br>2. How will we be informed? | This meeting is to discuss the following:<br><br>1. When is the new projected completion date?<br><br>2. How will we be informed? |

# ‖ Tip #44 ‖

## Avoiding a Festive Season Email Disaster

## The Challenge

During the year, no matter where you live and to which faith you belong, there are often two or three festive holidays. At these times it's easy to let our hair and email etiquette down, and maybe end up starring in the latest emailgate media disaster. Loose-lipped email messages can cause immense problems for the individual and the business. Reputations which take years to build and develop can be destroyed in a nanosecond at the press of a button.

The question many people ask us is, 'How can I loosen my style of writing whilst maintaining a business-like approach of which I can still be proud'.

## The Solution

Here are six top tips to help you lighten up as a festive season approaches whilst maintaining a highly professional image.

1.  Never email under the influence of drink when your judgement and vision could be impaired, such as before, during or after a festival event like Thanksgiving, Christmas, or Diwali.

2. Delay sending any email messages by at least two minutes. Either manually save them as drafts or write a rule to delay sending by two minutes. (See Avoid an Email Disaster.)

3. Add a sentence of best wishes/season's greetings, by all means, but that's it. Leave all the cosy ones for social email messages ('hiya', kisses and emoticons). Using 'season's greetings' reduces the risk of offending the recipient, who might not be celebrating the same festivity as you. If you know the other person's preference, then by all means use the appropriate festive greeting, but only when it is a one-to-one email.

4. Keep your Out of Office message safe and simple. Minimise the information available to prying eyes. Cybercriminals don't stop over the holiday period. In fact, the opposite is more likely, in the hope of finding a sloppy email.

5. Be extra judicious of email messages you receive with special offers. There is no such thing as a free lunch. An extraordinarily tempting offer is as likely as not, a phishing attempt.

6. Monitor when colleagues and friends tag you in a social media post, especially one showing you wearing a silly hat or performing interpretive dance when that is not your strong suit. You can delete your own post. However, theoretically, you have no control over what others post, except to politely request they take down images of you which might not do your reputation any good. There are settings which require your permission to be tagged. At some point you might be looking to change jobs, recruit more clients, or build your network. What is the first port of call for most people these days? Your internet footprint.

Although these tips are focused on email and social media behaviour during the festive season, they clearly apply at all times, but somehow when we approach and are immersed in festive events there is a psychological feeling that we can relax. This is fine. But just remember that bad email has a tendency to turn up when you least expect it. Once sent, your email will be out there somewhere for life.

# Tip #45

## Juggling the Inbox on the Road

### The Challenge

Prior to the Covid 19 pandemic, many PAs and EAs would pick up their email on the move, whether travelling, in between meetings or just nipping out for a coffee. There is no doubt once the norm is established, we will be on the road again, but maybe not quite so extensively. The challenges remain the same.

- First, deciding how best to deal with the inbox using multiple devices and particularly mobile ones when away from the 'normal' office desktop, and especially making sure you do re-read the message multiple times on different devices.
- Second, is it wise to be constantly connected?
- Third, picking up messages whilst on the road often means you are multi-tasking, something we know reduces productivity and may lead you to reply in haste and regret at leisure.

### The Solution

Over the last few years, mobile email apps have greatly improved, making synchronisation easier, and include more of the efficiency functions available on the full desktop client. There are two aspects to how best to handle your inbox on the road. The processes you use and the technology.

## Processes

The key is to ensure you don't read and re-read the same message on the road and then back at the desk without taking any action the first time you see it. This is just a waste of time. Here are nine tips to help you save time managing the inbox on the road and use this time wisely.

*Do you even want to pick up messages on the road?*

1. Decide whether or not you will deal with messages whilst on the road. Many top executives actually use the time away from the office for thinking, something we have so little time to do but which is a crucial part of being productive. Having an email message detox can be very good for both your wellbeing and productivity – see Email Detox - Five Tips to Disconnect.

2. If it is a really important message, you might need time to consider how to respond rather than making an instant response. You will also want no avoid typos.

3. Assuming that you do not wish to pick up messages whilst on the road, use the Out of Office (OOO) message to help you create no-message time. However, do provide an alternative way for people to contact you if they need you urgently. See Communicating 'Urgent' and 'Out-of-Office Replies - Overcoming the Hidden Dangers'.

*If you decide to juggle email messages on the road then how can you do it efficiently?*

1. Make time in your day to focus on the inbox even if it's only 10 minutes between meetings. Build this time into your

schedule. If you cannot, then it might be better not to check the mailbox at all and wait until there is a proper gap rather than reply hastily and make an error.

2. Set up a signature which allows for typos. For example, add a line such as 'Sent from my iPhone' or, 'Please excuse typos as I'm sending this whilst on the road'.

3. The 4Ds rule applies – action any message you read the first time around and do one of the following – Deal, Delete, Delegate or Defer. See 'Handle Each Email Only Once – The Four Ds Principle'.

4. Have a process which allows you to see clearly which messages you have dealt with, which you have not and to which you have sent a holding response. The most popular ones for use on mobile devices are:

   • Mark as unread those needing your attention when back in the office.
   • Set up a specific folder and move the message to it.
   • Flag the message.

5. For an important but long message, you could ask the sender which parts really need your attention immediately.

6. If you are going to be out for several days, use rules to filter out all the non-essential messages (for example, newsletters, cc'd messages, and systems notifications.) We both have many rules set up which can be switched on and off according to where we are for any length of time. For instance, When I'm away from the office for several days, all the newsletter rules are switched on. See Tips 'Outlook Rules Rule!' and 'Rules Rule: Gmail Filters' as well as 'Inbox Highway' for help on these techniques.

## The Technology

Gmail and Microsoft Outlook have added many functions which can be accessed on your mobile devices to help you manage your inbox more efficiently whilst on the road. Make sure you use them. Here are our top favourites.

Tips 1 through 5 assume you are using the full Outlook app rather than the email app native to your mobile device.

1. Use the Focused Inbox setting. This should show you only messages from key contacts. Occasionally you have to teach Outlook who is important/not important, but by and large it learns quickly. To change the priority, open the message, tap on the More menu (…) and select Move to Other.

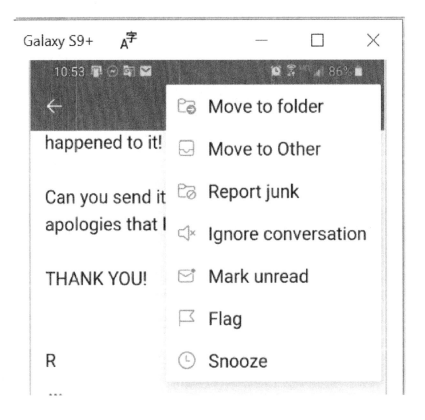

You are then prompted as to whether it is just the one message or messages always from that sender. See below:

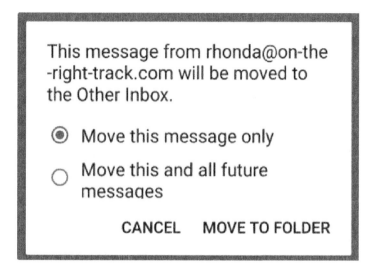

2.  Filter messages according to whether they are flagged, unread or have an attachment. Tap the Filter icon on the top right side of the screen and pick from the menu. See below.

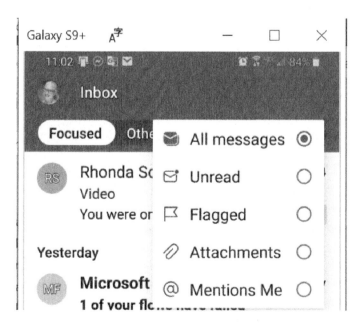

3. By conversation or not? By default, Outlook groups messages by conversation. To change this, go to Settings, and navigate to the Mail section and toggle 'Organize mail by thread' off.

4. To find items (such as messages and meeting invites) from specific people, use the search function at the bottom of the screen (magnifying glass).

5. Hear your messages spoken to you. There are two ways to do this:

   • Mac iOS users can ask Siri to 'read my email messages' or in the US 'play my email messages'.

   • Windows users have Cortana.

These are still in their infancy. The positives are that certainly Play My Email Messages (which is based on Cortana) can tell you how long the message is, when it arrived and if there are lots of images, hence a message better read on screen. The main downsides of this approach area that currently you cannot action the message and, if done whilst driving, it can be distracting. Definitely a technology to watch as it develops, and the apps allow you to do more sophisticated tasks like accept a meeting invite and move messages to folders.

But be warned: there is the temptation to have them read to you when driving. This is an absolutely no-go area as it is dangerous. Although hand-free use of the phone is still allowed, there are many who feel that even that should be banned because you are not paying full attention to driving.

6. In Gmail on your mobile device, star messages by tapping the star icon when you are checking messages on the go. Then, when you return, click the dropdown menu in Search, and in the Search field, toward the bottom of the dialogue box, select Starred. The most recent will appear at the top.

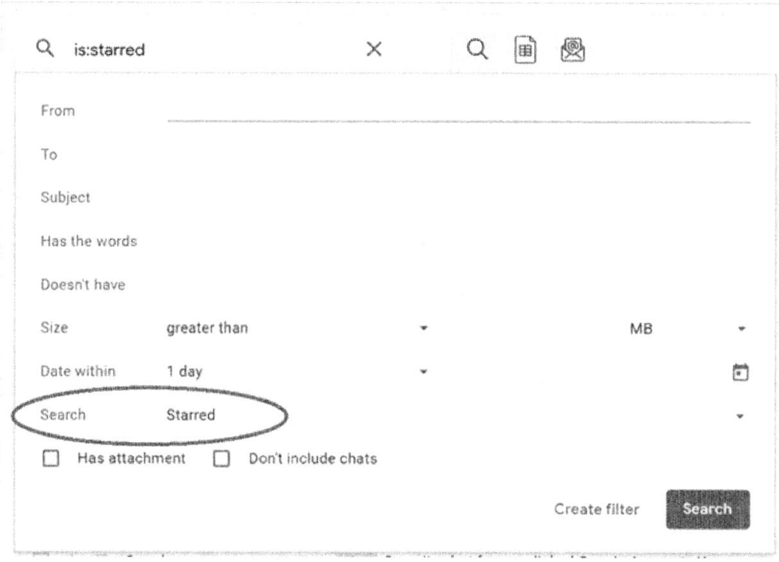
is:starred
From
To
Subject
Has the words
Doesn't have
Size
greater than
MB
Date within
1 day
Search
Starred
Has attachment
Don't include chats
Create filter
Search

# Tip #46

## Rules Rule: Gmail Filters

## The Challenge

If you've spent any time googling how to sort your email messages in Gmail, especially if you're coming from an Outlook shop, it can be pretty frustrating. While there is no facility to sort, per se, in Gmail, you can get quite a bit done with filtering. When you think about why you want to sort, it is usually to locate a particular message or set of messages from one individual or on a particular subject.

## The Solution

Create Filtering Rules With Gmail Filters.

From Search

At the top of the message list in Gmail is the Search field. If you find yourself searching for the same thing over and over, before you just go to the messages you found, click the down arrow at the right of the Search field and create a filter. Complete any additional criteria and click the link at the bottom right. Now you can star it, label it, forward it - almost any normal action you would take. When you've chosen the desired action, click the Create Filter button at the bottom left of the dialogue box.

If you change your mind at any point, click the 'x' in the upper right corner of the dialogue box. To clear the filter, click the inbox again. You can also start from a blank filter template by just clicking the dropdown arrow in the Search field and completing the fields manually.

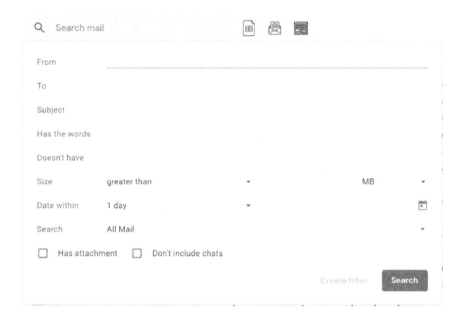

## Filter Actions

When you choose to create a filter, you must decide what should be done when the filter criteria are met. Here are some choices and how they can be best used.

- Skip the inbox and archive directly. Use this for messages you don't intend to read but need to hang on to for reference. To avoid creating more clutter, don't use this selection for  messages you should really delete.
- The Delete It choice is great for messages you don't want but technically are not spam  (for example, if a co-worker sends

information about social activities in which you have no interest).

- Starring an email (*) can give it high visibility in the inbox. Use this for messages for which you need to take action.

- Categorizing email messages allows you to group them into the tabs you see at the top of your message list, such as Personal, Social, Promotions, Updates and Forums.

- Labelling email displays all messages in a conversation with the label keyword. It also creates a way to quickly see only messages with that label by clicking the label name in the navigation list. Labels are roughly equal to folders, except that you can apply multiple labels.*

*A filtering rule cannot apply more than one label or star. You may write multiple filters to accomplish this.

If you want to apply your rule right now to everything in the inbox, don't forget to check 'Also apply filter to xx matching conversations'.

← When a message is an exact match for your search criteria:

☐ Skip the Inbox (Archive it)

☐ Mark as read

☐ Star it

☐ Apply the label: Choose label... ▾

☐ Forward it    Add forwarding address

☐ Delete it

☐ Never send it to Spam

☐ Send template: Choose template... ▾

☐ Always mark it as important

☐ Never mark it as important

☐ Categorize as: Choose category... ▾

☐ Also apply filter to **21** matching conversations.

❷ Learn more                                    Create filter

## Managing Filters

From the Settings gear, choose the Settings option. Along the top, you'll see a link to Filters and Blocked Addresses. Here, you will see a list of your filters and have the ability to edit or delete them.

# Settings

General    Labels    Inbox    Accounts    Filters and Blocked Addresses

Advanced    Offline    Themes

**The following filters are applied to all incoming mail:**

☐       Matches: **Google Payments**
        Do this: Star it

☐       Matches: **monday.com**
        Do this: Apply label "Collaborative Platforms"

☐       Matches: **Google Ads**
        Do this: Star it

# | Tip #47 |

## Creating Email Templates in Gmail

## The Challenge

There are three ways to send an email message that has the same contents as ones you send often. You can type it over again from scratch. You can search for an old message, then copy and paste the contents to a new message. The first method is a potential time waster. Doing repetitive tasks should always set off an alert for you to seek more efficiency. In the second method, there's always the danger of leaving non-relevant content in the new email message - for example, sending the same message to Iris that you sent to George, and accidentally leaving the salutation as 'Hi George!' The third method is to create templates that can be used over and over.

## The Solution

Gmail makes the creation and use of templates a breeze. (Even easier than in Outlook!)

- Simply compose your email message. Don't address it.

> **Pro Tip:**
>
> If you intend to use a friendly salutation, such as 'Hello', end it with a full stop (period) or exclamation point if that is your normal style. That way if you forget to put in the name, it won't be grammatically incorrect as it would be if you had typed it as 'Hello, <NAME>!'

- Look for the vertical ellipses (More options) at the bottom of the message window and choose Templates.

- From the fly-out menu, choose Save draft as template.

- Name it something easily recognisable.

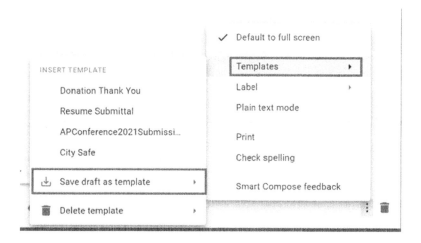

To use your template:

1. Click the Compose button in the navigation pane as you normally would to create a new message.

2. Click the More options ellipses at the bottom of the message as you did in Step 2 above.

3. Choose Templates.

4. Select the template you wish to use.

To delete a template you have created, follow Steps 2-3 above, then Delete template. You will be presented with a list from which to choose.

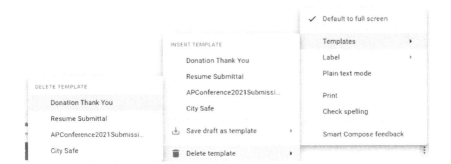

# Tip #48

## Using Categories, Stars and Labels in Gmail

## The Challenge

Gmail offers three ways to organise your email and stay on top of important tasks that come to you through email. But, which things do you use for what?

## The Solution

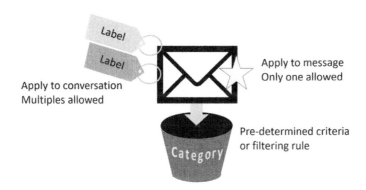

## Categories

When email first arrives in the inbox, it is examined by Gmail to see if it meets certain criteria. These are 'out of the box' and those conditions you set in a filtering rule. By default, Gmail will route messages to these categories based on the following information.

- *Primary:* From people you know and 'other'
- *Social:* From social networks
- *Promotions:* Deals, offers, newsletters
- *Updates:* Notifications, receipts, bill statements
- *Forums:* From online groups, discussion boards and mailing lists

These can also be 'learned' by Gmail as you drag and drop messages to the category tabs at the top of your screen. You can also star or label a message you have categorized in this way, but if you star it, it will appear both in the category you chose and the Primary category along with your other email. The message only exists once but appears in two places. Keep in mind that as of the writing of this book, creating custom categories is not an option.

## Stars

When looking at a list of messages in Gmail, you'll notice an empty star shape to the left of each one. If you click it, the star will change to the default colour yellow. If you have set up multiple stars to use, continuing to click the star will change the colour as you click. You set up multiple stars in Settings.

1. Click the settings gear at the top right of the window.
2. Choose 'See all settings'.

3. Scroll down in General settings to the Stars section.
4. Choose a preset number of stars and/or drag stars from the 'Not in use' line to the 'In use line.'

## Settings

General    Labels    Inbox    Accounts and Import    Filters and Blocke(

Add-ons    Chat and Meet    Advanced    Offline    Themes

messages arrive)
Learn more

| Stars: | **Drag the stars between the lists.** The stars will rotate in |
| | To learn the name of a star for search, hover your mous( |
| | Presets:    1 star   4 stars   all stars |
| | **In use:**    ☆  ★  ▦  ★  ☆  ☆  ✔  ? |
| | **Not in use:**    ☆  ‼  »  ! |

It is very important to remember that a star only applies to a single message and not a whole conversation. If you find that your strategy for prioritisation applies more to conversations than single messages, consider labels for priority instead.

## Labels

Labels function similarly to folders. The label names appear in the navigation pane on the left. Just like a message can be both categorized and starred, causing it to appear in both places, a message may be labelled with multiple labels. Do keep in mind that a label will apply to all messages in a conversation. The entire thread will be accessible when you click on the navigation pane label item.

As you click on the label in the navigation pane, you will see a message with more than one label appear in each one. The message actually only exists once in your Gmail mailbox. One useful feature of labels is the ability to assign colours to them, giving you a useful visual cue without reading the text of the label. Apply colors strategically to make prioritising or classifying your messages more straightforward. To change the colour of a label, click the vertical ellipses to the right of the label in the navigation pane and choose Label colour.

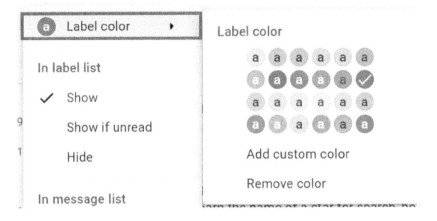

## The Right Strategy

You may choose to use one or all three of these techniques to organize your messages; however, approaching it with a well-thought-out strategy will make organising your email more effective. For example, you might choose to:

- Label by project or topic
- Star for action or priority
- Categorize for a tidy inbox

You can automate the assignment of these different tags using a filtering rule. See 'Rules Rule – Gmail Filters' for more information on how to set these up.

# Tip #49

## Tips for Working on Gmail Mobile

## The Challenge

As much as we like our desktop apps to work the same on a mobile platform, like a smart phone, there are just certain things that we need to operate differently on a smaller device. Preference aside, the inherent differences in the technologies mean that some things simply won't work the same, even when it seems they should. It can be quite frustrating to change from a desktop or laptop device to a smartphone, but Google has endeavored to make a few things easier.

## The Solution

Here are five things to know about working with Gmail on your mobile device that can make your life a little easier.

### Formatting Text

You might think you don't have the option to input anything other than plain text. However, if you just select your text and then double-tap the text and select Format from the pop-up, you'll see a rich text toolbar appear at the bottom of your message window offering bold, italic, underline, highlight colour and a clear formatting button that looks like a T with a slash through it. The process is similar on an iPhone, but you will scroll through your formatting options.

## Fat Finger Repellent

As soon as you're forced to work on a smaller screen with smaller buttons, you will inevitably click on something you didn't mean to and cause something to happen you didn't intend. In the Gmail mobile app, in Settings (general category), at the bottom you will see three handy checkboxes. Check them!

- Confirm before deleting
- Confirm before archiving
- Confirm before sending

## Message Order Without Interference

Google likes to 'help' you by placing things in the Promotions tab in the order it thinks is important rather than chronologically. Help it to stop helping you by going into Settings and choosing your email account. Select Inbox categories, then scroll to the bottom. Here you will find Enable Bundling of Top Email under the Promotions Tab section. Uncheck it. Now email messages in your Promotions tab will appear in chronological order.

## A Little Less Help, Please

If you have enough people (and apps) nagging you and telling you what to do, you can remove at least one of these in Gmail. Head to Settings again and choose your email account. Scroll down to Reply and followup under the Nudges section. Here you can uncheck one of both of these.

- *Suggest email messages to reply to* – Email messages you might have forgotten to respond to will appear at the top of your inbox.
- *Suggest email messages to follow up on* – Sent email messages you might need to follow up on will appear at the top of your inbox.

## Out of Office on Mobile

If you forgot to set your out-of-office responder before you left the office, you can do it on your mobile. Google snuck this feature in while we weren't looking. In Settings again, choose your email account. Scroll down and look for the Vacation responder. Tap the slide button to the on position and type your subject and message. The lesson of the Vacation responder is to always check out what's new in your apps. Google is always trying to improve things, but what they improve doesn't always get shouted from the rooftops.

# | Tip #50 |

## Mail Merge in Gmail

## The Challenge

Using the bcc: line to send the same message to multiple people may not be your best option. First, many spam filters will redirect your message to the trash folder of the recipient if it has too many addressees. It might even quarantine it and not send it at all. Second, it may not reflect well on your email skills. And last but not least, you can't really personalise the message for multiple people.

## The Solution

You could work with an email management program like Constant Contact or MailChimp. Or you could just use a simple add-on in Gmail. There are quite a few to choose from. In this chapter, we'll look at YAMM or Yet Another Mail Merge.

## Preparation

1.  To add the add-on, open Sheets (yes, Sheets!). This will enable Sheets to create your source data list to use in your mail merge.
2.  From the Add-ons dropdown menu, choose Get add-ons.
3.  Search for YAMM and click it when it appears.

Search results for YAMM

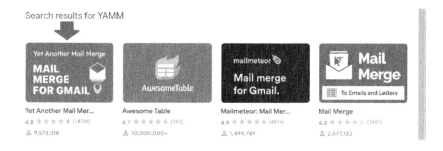

4. Choose either Domain Install (if you are the Google Workspace administrator) or Personal Install, confirm permission for the installation to continue and select your account. The personal installation will allow you up to 1,500 email messages a day, 50 recipients per message.

5. Test it. You will be prompted to either Import Google Contacts or Add data yourself. To try it out, choose Add data yourself. It will automatically populate the spreadsheet with your email address.

6. Open Gmail and create and save a test email template by composing a message and leaving off the addressees. (see Creating Email Templates in Gmail). You can name it YAMM TEST to easily identify it.

7. Return to Sheets and the Add-ons menu. You'll now see Yet Another Mail Merge on the dropdown menu. Select it and Start Mail Merge.

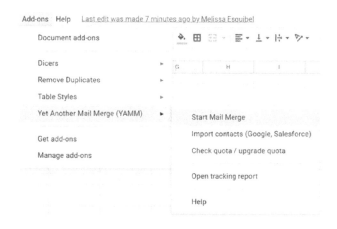

8. This will prompt you to select a template to use. Choose your YAMM TEST template. You will see this message when it is complete.

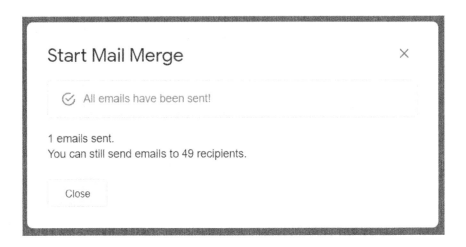

9. Check your inbox. You should see the email.

Now you're ready to do this for real.

## Create and Save Your Email Template

1. Compose a new message and leave off the addressees. Just populate the subject and the body.

2. To personalise each email message, use the << >> symbols to enclose the field name that you will have in your spreadsheet. For example, this is the spreadsheet we will ultimately create:

| | A | B | C | D |
|---|---|---|---|---|
| 1 | Email Address | First Name | Company | Donation |
| 2 | info@sawbuckseminars.com | Sharon | Sawbuck Seminars | $50 |
| 3 | howdy@melissaesquibel.com | Jack | MPELLC | $75 |
| 4 | mpellc@ripco.com | Melissa | Ripco | $30 |
| 5 | monica@mesmo.co.uk | Monica | MESMO Consultancy | $100 |
| 6 | | | | |

Therefore, our email template might look like this.

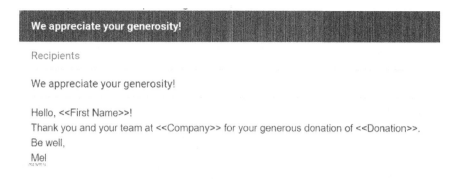

This one was saved as Donation Thank You. Make sure the field names in the brackets match EXACTLY the way you create them in Sheets.

3.  Open Sheets and create your spreadsheet as shown above.

4.  From the Add-ons menu, choose Yet Another Mail Merge and Start Mail Merge.

5.  Choose the template you just created above.

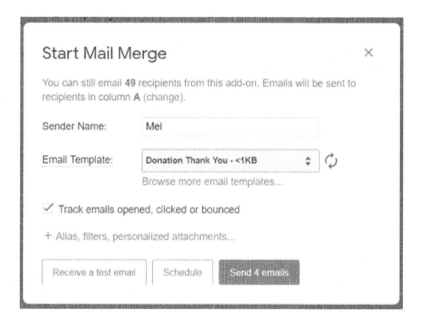

6. Confirm you want to send the email messages. If you like, you can test it first.

7. Save the Sheets file to track what happens to the messages after they go out.

Here is an example of what was received by one of the recipients:

## Donation Thank You

Hello, Sharon!
Thank you and your team at Sawbuck Seminars for your generous donation of $50.
Be well,
Mel

# Tip #51

## Not Now: Using Delay Features in Gmail for Sending and Receiving

## The Challenge

You are crafting a response to an important message at the end of the day. You know that if you send it now, it will be buried beneath the dozens of email message the recipient will see first thing in the morning. Probably best to send it an hour after she arrives and has gone through the first load of email. Another challenge might be that you are asking someone to do a task which is due a week from now. You also know that it might be lost in the shuffle of other work that busy person has to do. You will likely need to send a reminder, but will you remember to do that when it's time? After all, you are pretty busy yourself!

## The Solution

Gmail has a great solution for both of these circumstances called Schedule send, and it is very simple to use.

1. After you have composed and addressed your email message, in the bottom toolbar of the message window, you'll see the Send button. You may have never noticed that it has a drop

down button. If you click the drop down button, you'll see the option, 'Schedule send'.

2. When you click it, you will see this dialogue pop up. Choose from the offered times or click 'Pick date and time' for a selector that lets you choose from a calendar and specify an exact time.

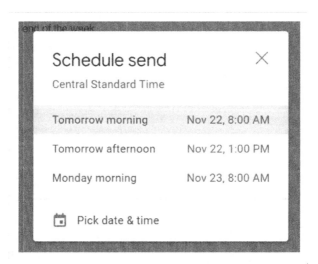

3. Once it's been scheduled, you can review the message or change your mind from this pop-up in the lower left corner of the Gmail window.

4. If you change your mind later about sending the message, you can click on Scheduled in the navigation pane. From there, you can choose Cancel Send.

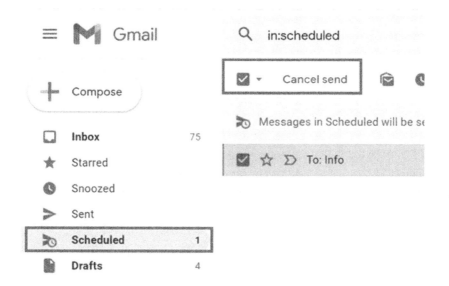

# TEAMWORK AND TASKS

# Tip #52

## Flags or Tasks for Reminders?

### The Challenge

What is the best way to keep track of important email messages which still require your attention? There are two similar ways: either add a reminder flag or create a task. Which is better?

### The Solution

Neither one is better. It is about:

- Personal preference
- How much time you spend out of the office looking at your inbox on a mobile device
- Whether or not you are managing another person's inbox
- Level of added data you need about the reminder

If a reminder date is set, both will generate a pop-up box on your desktop (Mac and Windows). However, there are some subtle differences, as shown in the following table.

| Process | Pros | Cons |
|---|---|---|
| Flags | Quick and easy. If you add a Reminder date, they will be added to your Task List, even if the reminder is 'No due date'. You can see all flagged items in the 'For Follow Up' Search Folder. | On a mobile device you must be able to see the Flagged Search Folder. For iOS users you need to add this as follows: Open the Mail app. Tap Edit in the upperright corner. Select Flagged. Tap Done. If you also use the Task List, this can become very cluttered. |
| Create a Task | Excellent if you like working from task lists. You can add notes and other rich content (see diagram below). You can assign the task to someone else. They turn red after their due date. If you are sharing your inbox or looking after another person's task list, you can see the complete list. | You need to complete the Task dialogue box. Takes about 15 to 30 seconds longer than adding a Flag. On an iOS mobile device, the task list does not automatically show up. You must add either the 'Reminder' or 'To Do' app. The latter is the more sophisticated. |

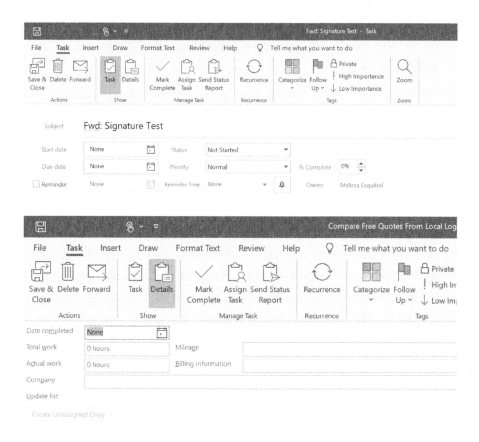

*Creating a Task from an Email – Information You Can Add.*

There is no right or wrong: it is a personal preference. Case in point: one of the authors prefers Flags, the other, creating Tasks. One is a Mac/iOS user, the other PC/Android.

# | Tip #53 |

## Forward an Email as a Task With a Reminder

## The Challenge

'I often need to forward time-critical email messages to a colleague for additional information before I can either reply to the original sender or complete a task (for example, prepare a report for the board). Despite adding an "Action By" date in the subject line, my colleague is frequently late in replying. This wastes time as we play email ping-pong, with me resending the original email. Furthermore, sometimes the task becomes both urgent and high priority and the situation is then quite stressful. Is there another way I can alert them to respond on time?'

## The Solution

Yes. You can either forward the email with a reminder flag or as a task and in both cases, it will turn red after the due date. For Windows Outlook users, this is how to do it.

### Forward an Email With a Reminder

1.  Either open the email to forward the email in the usual way or right-click and select Forward.

2. Click on the Follow Up icon, select Add Reminder and complete the dialogue box as required.

## Forward the Email as a Task

1. Drag and drop the email on your Task List.

2. Click on Assign Task (in the Manage Task block).

3. Complete the dialogue box as appropriate.

4. To add a reminder, click on the Follow Up icon and proceed as above.

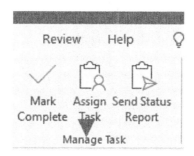

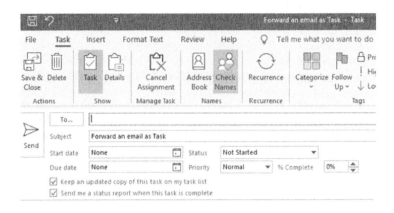

## *Mac Outlook*

You need to add the Follow Up reminder in the original email, then forward it. You might also add an Action By date in the subject line as an added reminder.

To send it as a Task, you must first drag and drop it on your own task list. Then you can forward it with a reminder. It is a two-step process rather than the one for Windows users.

## *Gmail*

In Gmail, tasks are not shareable. Clicking the task button will create a task for you, not the other person. You can forward the message and schedule when it can be sent for a little bit of help. Another option is to copy and paste the content of the email message to Keep. Keeps are shareable.

---

**Pro Tip:**

First, always set the reminder for at least two days before your personal deadline to allow the other person to fit it into their schedule.

Second, agree with the other person that this is how you will work with them to avoid missing important deadlines. If you don't and just insert reminders, it can be seen as aggressive rather than assertive email behaviour and might therefore backfire on you.

---

# Tip #54

## Using Favourites to Manage High Priority Items

### The Challenge

Do you try to manage your high priority items by keeping them marked as unread? This is fine in a low volume inbox. But if you're one of those whose inbox seems to be more like a firehose of information, this method may become untenable.

### The Solution

By creating folders and Search Folders (see 'Don't make copies of email messages' as well as 'Rules to route messages to appropriate folders' (in Outlook Rules Rule!), then adding those folders to your Favourites, you can use the unread flags to alert you of what's new and important and why.

When you add a folder to your favourites, it will always show the count of unread messages. So, for example, if you have a rule which routes customer inquiries to a folder called the same, you will see the number increment each time a new, unread message comes through. That way, you can avoid having to discern whether something new and important comes through. Your favourites can tell you this with folders like these:

- Customer Issue
- New Business
- From 'Executive Name'
- Reply by COB (close of business)

You can also layer on the use of Categories and create a Search Folder for those such as:

- Routed to 'Colleague Name'
- Waiting on Response
- Completed

Add the Search Folders which indicate status or priority to your favourites for a quick reference as to the status of your work in hand.

⌄ Favorites

___URGENT

BEFORE YOU LEAVE

Unread Mail                      113

Inbox - melissa@esquib...   113

Inbox - info@sawbucksemi...   2

# Tip #55

## Urgent Task to Complete?
## Make a Meeting With Yourself!

## The Challenge

I have an ongoing task list, but about once a week an item on my task list suddenly becomes urgent. The deadline has been approaching for several days but somehow there is always something else which needs doing on the day I intended to tackle the original task. The task has nearly always come either via an email or as the outcome of a meeting. Now I am faced with working late and under pressure to complete what is both an urgent and high priority task. Not good for either my wellbeing or work-life balance. How can I reduce the frequency of these stressful moments happening?'

## The Solution

Life is not perfect and there will always be times when an urgent task lands on your desk. This is about both managing your time better and using your electronic calendar more effectively.

## Managing Your Time Better

When you are given a task in the normal course of the working week, but which has a defined deadline, here are three simple steps to take to avoid them becoming both urgent and high priority.

1.  Make a meeting with yourself to do it. If it is a large and possibly complex task, break it up and make several such 'me meetings' to tackle each part.

2.  Set the meeting(s) for at least two days ahead of the deadline to build in time for the unforeseen.

3.  Use your electronic calendar to save time. If the task comes via an email, for Outlook users you have two options depending on whether or not the email has an attachment.

    a)  Hold the left button down, simply drag and drop the email on the calendar icon and it will open up a new appointment as shown below.

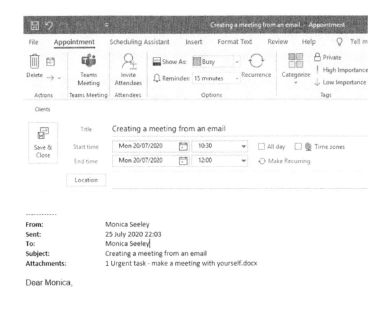

b) If the email has an attachment and you want to include it in the body of the appointment, hold the right button down and drag it to the calendar icon. From the menu, select 'Copy Here as Appointment with Attachment' (or hit the 'C' key). Then complete the details as normal. When you open the meeting you also have the attachment at hand, which saves you going back to the inbox.

## Mac Users

You can either use the drag and drop process or right-click and from the dropdown menu select Create/Appointment.

On the Mac, the default is to include the attachment. You might want to remove it, especially if you have mailbox limits. Otherwise you are using valuable space, because you are now effectively storing the attachments in two different places within your mailbox.

*Caution* – for Outlook users, whatever operating system you use (Mac or Windows), if you have an open calendar which anyone can see you might want to mark this meeting as private. This prevents others reading either the email or the attachment which might contain confidential/ sensitive information. They then just see that you are busy but no other details.

## In Gmail

You have a similar and a different option in Gmail.

1. You can click the ellipses at the top of an open mail message and choose to create an event. Just save it when the Event dialog pops up.

2. You can also 'snooze' an email to pop to the top of your list on a certain day by clicking the clock button in the toolbar just above the open message. It's not exactly as strong an action as carving out time on your calendar, but it will come to your attention when you want it to.

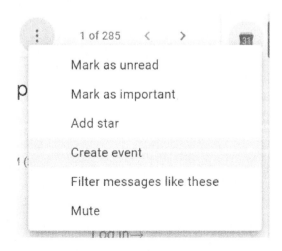

# Tip #56

## Notebook Apps Instead of Email

### The Challenge

Email overload is an issue. When we speak to administrative professionals, we hear of daily rates of email in the hundreds. While email will likely remain a popular way to communicate in business, less email to slog through certainly goes to productivity, time-savings and ability to focus on priority communications. Organisations are increasingly turning to robust platforms like Microsoft Teams, Slack, Trello and Asana (see Tip 65, 'Consider Collaborative Tools', page 226). However, shared notebooks in OneNote, Evernote and Keep may be an option for organisations who choose not to use these platforms or who need a simpler solution.

### The Solution

Many administrative professionals are using shared notetaking apps like OneNote, Evernote and Keep to communicate with the managers and executives they support. Here are three ways we've learned about from savvy admins who use notebook apps.

**Daily Binder** – These notebooks contain links or attachments to all of the materials needed to meaningfully lead or participate in meetings, interviews and appointments. OneNote and Evernote integrate well with Outlook, allowing for the depositing of meeting invitation information to a notebook page. To this, add presentations, documents and notes. You can use a section for the day and a page per meeting. In OneNote, you can create subpages beneath a page for additional information. You can add a 'To Do' page for various tasks, forms and calls that must be done on that day. In a shared Keep scenario in GoogleWorkspace (formerly G Suite), you are better off using a single Keep document for a day. There is limited capability to add different types of content, but you can certainly add links.

**Q&A on the Road** – When the people with whom you must communicate are on the road, instead of sending scores of email and text back and forth about important, but non-urgent matters, you might just as easily keep these issues in a running list on a notebook. If you use tags in either OneNote or Evernote to represent questions and answers, you can make time to search these tags several times a day to check for new queries and new information. Keep offers a 'to-do' list checkbox tag. It might suffice to put a checkbox next to questions and the person answering them, can check the box.

## Q&A - Tom & Melissa
Thursday, October 15, 2020      7:05 AM

? Did we remember to file the 986 form with the tax accountant?
▲ We did. This was filed on September 29, 2020
? I think I might need to extend my rental car another day. I'm going to stay over Friday night.
? I just got a question about our last prospectus, can you shoot over a PDF for me by tomorrow?
▲ Here's a link to the official version on the website. http://ourprospectus.co/2020Q3

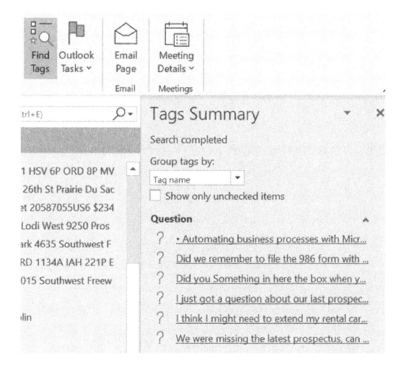

Consider using the idea tag for things you want to cover during your next one-on-one meeting, such as streamlining repeated one-off questions of a particular type. For example, an idea tag might go on the statement, 'I notice you frequently request our latest prospectus while you are on the road. Would you like me to simply include it on each trip page?'

**One-on-Ones** – Speaking of one-on-one meetings with your manager or executive, as topics come up during the week, keep them in a specific notebook. Send email messages, screenshots, questions, kudos, links to products available online, whatever you want to discuss. That way when you get that very valuable one-on-one time, you can quickly run through the items on your list without hesitation. You can share the page for that specific one-on-one with your executive moments before you meet so that you are both looking at the same information. If you don't want to share your personal notebook, you can email a page (OneNote) or copy and paste the text to a new email message.

# | Tip #57 |

## Use OneNote for Meeting Management

### The Challenge

I met an executive assistant who had a brilliant system for managing meetings using OneNote. Her challenge was in supporting multiple executives, all of whom mostly required her to plan and manage dozens of meetings and keep up with the throngs of email, meeting invitations, acceptances, queries, resources and preparations. She employed OneNote to keep it all straight. Here is how she did it.

### The Solution

1. Her OneNote notebook had a section (tab) for each executive she supported. As she would receive an email requesting that she set up a meeting, she sent it to OneNote in the section belonging to that executive. She would then delete the original email message from Outlook.

2. She renamed the page created in OneNote for the date, subject and time of the meeting - for example, '20200815-Teams Training'.

3. Time: 10 a.m-11 a.m.

4. New subpages were created with additional messages from the meeting sponsor about what was needed, who was required and any additional requirements.

5. Once meeting invitations were sent and responded to, she would put the final roster in as copied from the Tracking information. She created a rule to gather all the Accepts/Declines for review and deletion.

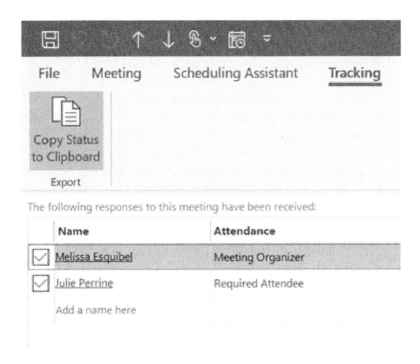

6. She would also put the prepared presentation deck here as a backup to what the executive had on his or her computer. In addition, another subpage was created for meeting notes.

7. After the meeting, with the meeting notes cleaned up, she could use the Email Page function of OneNote to send to all the attendees.

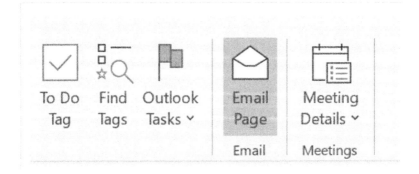

There are many ways to use OneNote to manage meetings. This is just one scenario which worked brilliantly for this EA. She reduced the amount of email in her inbox, had one place to which she could refer for all things about a single meeting and could archive the meeting (page and subpages) to another Archived section for future reference.

# | Tip #58 |

## Use OneNote for Meeting Minutes

### The Challenge

Love it or hate it, for many administrative professionals, taking minutes is an important part of their regular tasks. Where to take them and how, where to share them and how, and how to keep everything straight meeting to meeting can be an ever more challenging set of decisions. One solution is OneNote.

As of this writing, Microsoft has renamed OneNote 2016 to OneNote and maintains OneNote for Windows 10 as the version that ships with the PC operating system. Regardless of which one you have (or indeed whether you have either), OneNote Online remains accessible to anyone. To learn more or to change your installation see: https://support.microsoft.com/en-us/office/install-or-reinstall-onenote-for-windowsc08068d8-b517-4464-9ff2-132cb9c45c08. For minute-taking, we recommend the desktop version of OneNote.

### The Solution

If you've used OneNote before, you will be familiar with its structure.

- **Notebook** – The OneNote file.

- **Section** – Tabs at the top which collect groups of pages.

- **Page** – Where content is actually stored.

- **Subpage** – A subordinate page to group content under a main page. There are two levels of subpages available.

- **Links** – Within content, links can be created between notebooks, sections, pages and paragraphs of content as well as externally to websites.

- **Tags** – Metatags that help identify content visually while reading and which are searchable to retrieve content of a particular kind (for example, 'to do' items).

## Structure

This structure lends itself nicely to OneNote. The effectiveness of a OneNote solution is roughly equal to the amount of pre-work you do to make the minute-taking in the actual meeting easy. To that end, here is one methodology.

1. If you have a single body that meets regularly and requires that minutes be easily accessible from previous sessions, then whether or not you choose to share the notebook with the committee, board or team, a single notebook can be set up. Given the nature of confidentiality of proceedings for some bodies that meet, it is best to have at least a separate notebook for each one.

2. Sections can be defined for each meeting by date. It might be easiest to name them for YYYY-MM-DD to easily be able to arrange and refer to them. Additional useful sections which are used as resources might be:
   a) Members list
   b) Glossary
   c) Summary of bylaws or team rules as it relates to the frequency and conduct of meetings

3. For each meeting, several pages can be set up.

   a) Agenda – The email announcing the meeting can be copied here instead if it contains the agenda and the invited attendees.
   TIP: As amendments are made to the agenda, you can add subpages containing a copy of each email message on this subject.

   b) Actual minutes – A copy of the agenda as text to easily lay out areas in which to take the minutes. This should be the only area in which you should be active during the meeting.

   c) Published minutes - This can be further broken down into subpages called Attendance, Minutes, Follow-up Summary, Voting Summary and Items Tabled for Next Meeting.

4. Depending upon the size of the group, you may want to set up a custom tag for each member. This will help to identify their follow-up items, votes, actions, motions, and so on. You will also want easy tags to identify issues voted on, carried, rejected and tabled. Here is one example of a set of custom tags you could set up. Notice that the first nine will have shortcuts assigned to them. These are really handy on a PC. While you can use tags on the Mac and Online versions, they do not offer all the features that the PC desktop version does, such as short cuts and a printable Tag Summary.

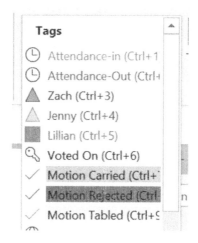

## Mechanics

## Attendance

After setting up the structure and including any planning content (agenda, email discussion of agenda items), it's time to take minutes.

This may also include taking attendance, especially when a quorum is needed to vote on issues. With the tags you set up previously, as people come into the room, you would type their first name or initials. For example, Zach walks in. Type Zach, then use Ctrl+1 to show it as 'Attendance-in'. Alt+Shift+T will time stamp the entry. Should Zach leave during the meeting to take a call or otherwise make himself unavailable for discussion and voting, you can once again type Zach, then Ctrl+2, followed by Alt+Shift+T to record the time he left. Repeat the first sequence when he returns.

Using the Find Tags button, you will have these types of summaries to verify attendance and quorum. Of course, they will also be in line with your minutes in text as well.

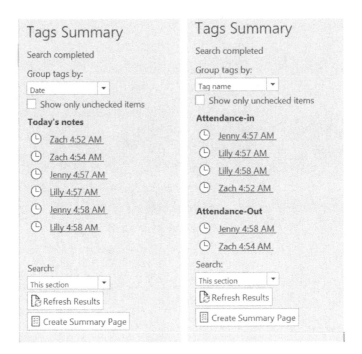

## Minutes

Depending upon the latitude you are given and/or the permissions granted to record the meeting, you could choose to put OneNote on 'autopilot' either by turning on the Record Audio feature or by launching Word and activating the Dictate function. *Be forewarned: recording audio in the workbook may cause problems if you are connected to cloud storage in the moment, as OneNote tries to save frequently to keep all your content.* It might be best to record locally using something like the Voice Recorder app to guarantee it will record locally. With at least one computer or window performing voice to text on a locally stored file or recording the actual audio, you are free to record only the pertinent pieces of the meeting: attendance, key discussion points, issues voted upon, outcomes of voting, calls to order, adjournment and points of parliamentary procedure for those following guidelines such as Robert's Rules of Order

It is not uncommon for the person taking notes not to necessarily be a subject matter expert in everything discussed. As you run across terms and acronyms you do not understand (but with which everyone else in the room seems to be comfortable), mark them for look-up with another tag such as the question tag or the idea tag. Then, afterwards, you can do your research and enter those items in the Glossary. Anything you had to look up, you can create a tag for by selecting the Glossary entry and right-clicking. Choose Copy Link to Paragraph. Then in your minutes, select the term and use the Ctrl+K shortcut (or right-click, Link) and paste the link. That way, you can quickly identify the context for understanding the term.

## Wrap-up

At the conclusion of the meeting, if you have used all your tags to identify follow-up items and who's doing what, clicking Find Tags should get you a quick summary of attendance, voting and follow-up tasks. If everyone agrees that it is a fair representation of what took place, then you can move on to refining and editing the minutes. You will hopefully have the text transcript and/or audio recording.

*A **word of caution:** All word-for-word text and recordings should be deleted once the minutes are refined and published; a good deal of discussion does not need to be memorialised, indeed SHOULDN'T be memorialised. Only the results, key points of discussion and voting are likely to be required. Anything additional might result in legal exposure for your organisation. Always be sure that all members agree to be recorded (in whatever form you use). If anyone dissents, it would, practically speaking, preclude you from recording anyone. While it might make your minute-taking a bit more labour intensive, in many jurisdictions it is a point of law which cannot be ignored.*

# ‖ Tip #59 ‖

## Use OneNote for One-On-One Meetings With Your Executive

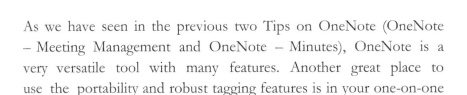

As we have seen in the previous two Tips on OneNote (OneNote – Meeting Management and OneNote – Minutes), OneNote is a very versatile tool with many features. Another great place to use the portability and robust tagging features is in your one-on-one meetings with the people you support.

## The Challenge

Whether you support one or several executives, it is a good idea to schedule regular one-on-one meetings to ensure you are working on the right things in the right way, and that you are aware of things coming up which might rock the priority boat. Once the meeting has ended, you are hopefully walking away with things to do. What happens if you have questions later? What if your executive forgot a key piece of information she later remembers? Do these items get lost in a sea of email? Using OneNote to memorialisze and hold follow-up content might be a good strategy.

# The Solution

To maintain the appropriate level of confidentiality between executives, create a one-on-one notebook for each one.

If you also maintain a personal notebook, you can create links to each of them in a list on one page to make them all easily accessible. Depending upon the volume of content you expect, you might want to create a page per week or a page per month.

The content you record need not be complex. Using tags can help you and your executive keep track of questions that need to be answered and offer a place to go to link to the result of a task. For example, the page might look like this.

The best part is if you both have access to the mobile app – these notebooks on your Office 365 cloud platform can be accessed anywhere! Rather than swimming through a sea of two-line email messages, checking the notebook at various times during the day will suffice to keep the information flowing smoothly long after the one-on-one.

# | Tip #60 |

## Apps to Save Internet Content to Read Later

## The Challenge

When looking for information on the internet, I often find content which I want to save for either reuse or reading later. Obviously, I can bookmark the site but then I end up with a very long list of bookmarks, and sometimes I want to read the material on another device and maybe even offline. The latter cannot be done and the former assumes one is using the same browser on all devices which is not always the case. What other ways are there to save web-based content for easy access anywhere, and especially reading offline?

## The Solution

There are several good apps which allow you to save content for reading later both on any device and off-line. The one best suited to you will depend on exactly what you want to do with the content. First, here is a list of the typical functions you might need.

### Typical Functions of Apps for Saving Internet Content

There are eight basic functions which such apps offer.

1. Save the content for reading anywhere, any time and on any device.
2. Organise the content you save into groups of similar content.
3. Listen to the content, for example, whilst walking or cycling.
4. Save and share the content.
5. Curate new content of specific themes.
6. Speed read the content.
7. Create favourites which can be quickly re-found.
8. Archive items that are not of interest at present.

## Choice of Apps

Most apps have a free version and will probably be suitable as a starting point. They all work in much the same way. You add the extension to your browser, create an account (or use an existing account such as Facebook or Gmail) and download the app to your mobile device. Our favourites which offer free versions are as follows.

1. Pocket – The most popular probably because it is one of the easiest to use. The free version lets you organise your content using 'tags', listen to content (when online), share it and save content from social media too. However, to do more you need a subscription - for example, to search your database of saved content and create favourites which can be easily re-accessed.
2. Instapaper – Aas popular as Pocket. The paid for version offers some additional functions such as speed reading and reading the text even if you are offline, has a Kindle interface for the Amazon eReader and allows you to change the font size.
3. Flipboard – Stored content can be organised into a story board format, which some find easier to read. Its strength is its ability to curate content from your interests, particularly from newspapers and magazines but for the more interesting ones you may have to pay a fee.
4. Emailthis.me – Aas its name suggests, it email messages you the content advert-free. The downside is that it drives up the volume of email traffic in your inbox. That aside, it's easy to use

but of course does not offer any search or grouping functionality.

5. Evernote – If you already use this electronic notebook app, this might be your first choice. Its Web Clipper function allows you to store the entire content and not just the link (like OneNote). You just need to install the Web Clipper extension to your browser. Very useful for working offline.

There are many others such apps which are only available for a subscription including: Pinboard, WorldBrain, and Raindrop.io. The best advice is to start with one of the above and then decide if there are some functions you must have, and which are only available elsewhere. However, make sure before you move apps that you can import all your content from the previous app. Also, you may find that the functions are in fact available on the subscription version and that if it costs just a little extra the money will be worth not having to make the effort of learning a new interface and way of working.

One of the great benefits of such apps is that they do not let you get distracted – See Managing Distractions.

# Tip #61

## Create a Desk Manual With OneNote

In previous OneNote tips, we've shown how to provide support to executives and groups who meet. In this tip, we offer a way for a team of administrative professionals to support each other.

## The Challenge

In an organisation with several administrative professionals, there is always the potential for duplication of effort or last-minute panic when one person has to cover for another. A desk manual for each administrative professional, or a single notebook with a section for each administrative professional, can go a long way to optimise the time spent when you need to support each other.

## The Solution

### Get Agreement

Have a gathering of the administrative professionals who will be participating in the Desk Manual Project. Get permission and agreement to share certain information between you regarding the people you support. In many cases, a complete 100% open agreement will be difficult to get.

However, these are only additional challenges that can be met with information stored outside of OneNote requiring specific access control permissions.

## Set Up Structure

You will want to agree on a structure. Here is a suggested structure for a single notebook with a section for each administrative professional.

1. Admin Wiki

   a) Supplies
   b) Phone system
   c) Conference rooms
   d) Other shared resources – Think about what a temp might need to know.

2. Melissa

   a) Executive Profile: Andrea

      i. Phone numbers
      ii. Family phone numbers
      iii. Email addresses
      iv. Residence address
      v. Upcoming travel
      vi. Current priority projects
      vii. Current 'block list' of people/vendors (take a message)

   b) Executive Profile: Lillian

      i. Phone numbers
      ii. Family phone numbers
      iii. Email addresses
      iv. Residence address

      v.    Upcoming travel

     vi.    Current priority projects

    vii.    Food allergies!!!

  c)  Executive Profile: Zach

       i.    Phone numbers

      ii.    Family phone numbers

     iii.    Email addresses

     iv.    Residence address

      v.    Upcoming travel

     vi.    Current priority projects

    vii.    Gym schedule (DND time!! Unless it's his wife or daughter, urgently)

Now any time one of you needs to sub in for the other, you'll be able to go to their page, review any upcoming travel or projects and ask pertinent questions about those things (instead of 'What's her husband's name? Does she have any food allergies? Are there times when she shouldn't be disturbed?'). Also, should you need to bring in a temp for a few days, you can create a document easily for your sections to leave as notes. Just click File, then Print and Print Preview and select to print the entire section, which would be all of the people you support. You can also print the Wiki section so that he or she will have the general information of how things in the office work among administrative professionals.

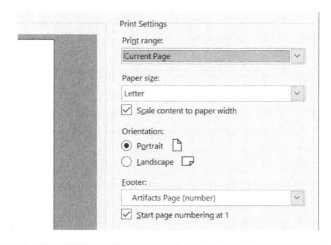

# | Tip #62 |

## Insert a Reminder in a Recipient's Email

### The Challenge

It's not unusual for business-people to receive 60+ email messages per day and spend much of their day in meetings. Specific colleagues often forget to reply to email messages on time. This may mean items go from being urgent to urgent and high priority; missing a deadline can be costly and creates unnecessary stress for everyone. How can you make sure they reply on time without appearing to nag them?

### The Solution

One way which works very well for many clients, is to insert a reminder. As with all such reminder techniques, it's important that you agree whatever on process you'll employ with the other person prior to using it: otherwise you risk coming across as arrogant and too clever by half!

1. Open a new email.

2. From the Tags menu group, click on Follow Up and select Custom from the dropdown menu.

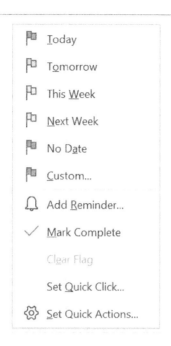

3.  In the Custom dialogue box, click on Flag for Recipients. Click on Reminder and set the date and time you want the recipient to be reminded. After that date the email turns red.

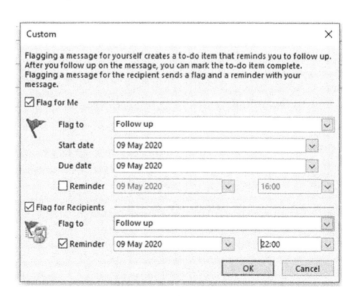

## Super user tip

What if you want the email to turn red immediately when it arrives in the recipient's inbox? Set the reminder date to a date and/or time before you send it.

If you include a Flag for Me (top half of the dialogue box), the reminder will also show up on your Task List.

# Tip #63

## Share the Load With Google Keep

### The Challenge

If you are a Google Workspace user, you know the struggle of being able to create tasks, but not share or assign them to others. If you are not using a third party app like Asana or Monday.com to distribute work, you are left with email, the glut that builds for follow-up messages and the back and forth of status checking. Is there another option?

### The Solution

Yes, there is! For tasks and small scale projects, you can use Keep. Google Keep is available to you by default in either Google Workspace or the free Google platform. Simply click on the app launcher (waffle) in the upper right corner of your Google window. You may need to scroll down within the apps shown to locate Keep.

1.  Open Keep.

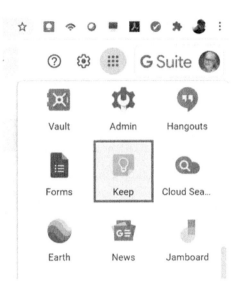

2. From the dashboard of Keep, you can just start typing in the 'Take a note…' field.

3. Title your note and list the tasks that need to be done.

4. To make tracking easier, click the More button (vertical ellipses) and choose Show checkboxes. As tasks are completed they will float down to the bottom and show as crossed off.

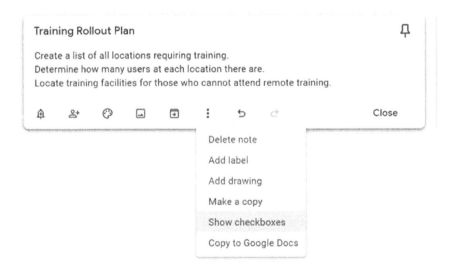

5. To add collaborators and effectively share the task list, click the Collaborator button at the bottom of the note. Invite people to participate with you on the task list.

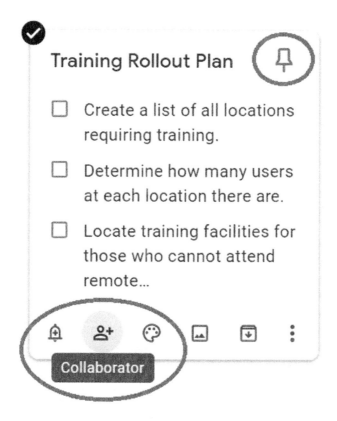

6. To keep current task lists top of mind and top of screen, use the thumbtack icon to pin them.

There isn't much more to Keep than this, but if this is all you need, you're good to go!

# ‖ Tip #64 ‖

## Getting the Flow to Go With YOU

## The Challenge

It is not uncommon anymore to have work teams that use different platforms for email, calendar, task management and document creation and storage. Keeping calendars straight between Google and Microsoft and remembering that new files added to OneDrive might not be on the radar for those that use Google Drive is challenging. Knowing that when someone adds a line to a Google Sheet, someone needs to take an action in some other app is also a challenge when trying to hold everything together and keep productive.

## The Solution

One solution might be to use a workflow app. One of the originals of this type of app was IFTTT, created in 2010. Others that came along are Zapier and Power Automate (Microsoft), which was formerly known as Flow. With these apps, a trigger, such as someone adding a line to a spreadsheet in Sheets or creating a calendar item in Microsoft 365 Calendar, would set off a follow-on action such as creating a task or creating a like calendar item in Google Calendar. Let's explore some popular ones and how they might be used to make your life easier even as the technology platforms you have to deal with get more complicated.

## IFTTT

Visit IFTTT.com and check out the free app that helps you connect multiple platforms with up to three workflows. More are available for a reasonably priced paid subscription. Just add a trigger, or an 'If This' and then specify the actions 'Then That'. As an example, this IFTTT notices when a new file is added to a Dropbox folder and sends an email from a Microsoft 365 Outlook account to someone who needs to take an action. It took about two minutes to set up.

## Zapier

In Zapier (Zapier.com), you create Zaps. Zapier work similarly to IFTTT in that you set up a trigger and an action. With Zapier paid version, you can connect things like PayPal or other online payment portals and put things like webinar registrations on autopilot. Here's an example of one used by Sawbuck Seminars to detect a successful payment in PayPal of a particular product code, which is determined only the 'Only continue if...' step and registers a participant for a webinar in Zoom.

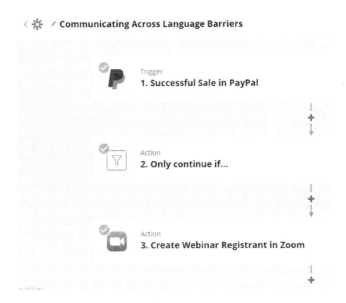

## Power Automate

Microsoft has an entry in this field of apps as well, and it is available in Microsoft 365 Business subscriptions. First introduced as Flow, Power Automate continues to grow in its capacity to manage multiple actions in multiple app platforms. It also has several templates from which to start that can address many common needs. For example, when an event is added to Google Calendar, it can create a like item in an Outlook calendar.

## Getting Started

Experiment with these tools to see how many tasks you can eliminate with automation. Check out the tutorials for each available from the vendor. Then explore YouTube! Getting the lowdown on using these tools from actual users will alert you to the occasional 'gotcha' and help you envision how best to get started. Start with simple connections and actions first. Then, as you get more adept, create multistep flows to automate even more tasks. If you find that the apps you want to connect aren't available, just know it's probably more like not yet. All of these apps are always expanding what they can do.

# Tip #65

## Consider Collaborative Tools

## The Challenge

At the time of writing this book, one of the most talked about groups of apps is collaborative tools. These are designed to improve communications and information sharing. To some extent, these are not new. Some popular ones have been around for almost two decades. Initially, they were often referred to as 'groupware'. Now, they have become easier to use and are often promoted as the solution to email overload. In the case of apps such as Microsoft Teams, they are sold as part of the Microsoft suite and can be on your desktop. With the rise in working from home, more than ever we are asked, 'Should I be using one, and if so, which one?'

## The Solution

Like all software and apps, they are only useful if you have a business problem which they can help you solve. Today's collaborative tools come in all shapes and sizes and thus offer a huge variety of functionality, from simple file sharing to facilitating a group sing-a-long with video-conferencing. They can do practically anything but make a coffee.

The initial stage is to look at the real problem you are trying to solve. Is it one, some or all of the following?

## Typical Functions

There are seven basic functions which such tools offer.

1. File sharing
2. Video conferencing
3. Project management
4. Team management and performance
5. Information management and sharing
6. Text messaging
7. Discussions

All of the above involve communications and are often done via email. This may be why so many people suffer with chronic email overload. Email is not always the right, nor the most effective, communications channel. Collaborative tools are increasingly being used to replace internal email both within organisations and across self-contained, external working groups.

## Choice of Tools

As with the discussion on apps for saving and curating internet sites (see Pocket app for saving internet articles you don't have time to read), there are so many collaborative tools that writing about them could fill a book in itself. In addition to the process you are trying to improve, you also need to factor in:

- The devices across which you want to use it;
- Whether it is intended for internal or external communication, or a mix.

Here is a summary of the most commonly used apps at the time of writing. These currently work on most devices and operating systems (iOS and Windows).

1. Microsoft Teams. A current market leader, Teams is included as part of Microsoft 365 Business licences. It offers file sharing, video conferencing, text messaging, and chat board for discussion. Its main strength is its ability to connect to other apps and online services both within and external to the Microsoft group of products. For more information, see 'Teams Rather Than Email'. It can be cumbersome to work with people external to your organisation. Though Teams does allow it, it is a setting which is governed by the Microsoft 365 administrator. Many IT groups are hesitant to crack this door open, even a little. If the deployment of Teams is not well thought out, it can also be hard to know where certain information is located.

2. Slack, which preceded Teams, offers the same type of functionality and many think it is easier to use. A primary argument in choosing Slack over Teams is that it is an additional component to your productivity platform which is outside the Microsoft 'ecosystem.' If this is not a concern, then ease of use-might nudge Slack ahead of Teams.

3. Asana. In a head-to-head comparison between Asana and Slack, there is little difference. In 2008, when it was created, it had very little competition. Like its competitors, it allows you to share information and files, track and assign tasks and communicate with other team members. Again, there is no video-conferencing feature, but it integrates with Teams and Zoom. It also works on all devices and platforms.

4. Monday.com does what many of these other tools do, but really shines in the area of managing workflows among team members. It is easily customisable, aesthetically pleasing and visually easy to understand. It lacks the communications (voice,

real-time chat), but shines in process flows and efficiency. It also can be integrated with Teams.

5. Trello. Primarily a vehicle for sharing documents, ideas and discussions, it looks like a massive white-board with posted sticky notes. In Trello, these are known as Cards. It has no video capability, but is easy to use and facilitates the sharing of ideas. New cards and entries are dynamic and have additional features that lend themselves to task management. You can tag people, add comments, set up categories and more. Like Monday and Asana, it also integrates with Teams.

6. Dropbox. The ultimate file sharing collaborative tool. Does exactly what it says on the can. Dropbox has added more and more functionality over the years, including version management, commentary and the communication of changes to files. One of the better changes that has come to Dropbox is that you can edit documents in Microsoft Word within the Dropbox app. It is essentially file management, but is growing to accommodate the way we want to collaborate on documents.

7. OneNote. This app comes pre-installed with Windows 10 and is also available as a standalone desktop application. While originally put forth as a notetaking app like Evernote, it has grown into an all-encompassing repository with shareability and version control. With the use of tags and linking, OneNote becomes a viable place to collaborate on small to medium sized projects. It has some of the same drawbacks as Teams when it comes to sharing externally. Notebooks are stored in the Microsoft cloud and are governed by Microsoft 365 administrative choices. While notebooks are easy to collaborate on with a personal cloud storage account such as OneDrive, it may lead to circumventing established organisational information sharing policies. For more about using OneNote, see 'OneNote Meeting Management',

'OneNote Minutes', 'OneNote One-on-Ones', 'Create a Desk Manual With OneNote', and OneNote Instead of Email'.

Most of these tools offer a free version, albeit with limited functionality or a limit on the time to use it without paying. The best advice is to trial one or more of the above and then decide which has the functions you must have. If you decide to change platforms, determine what content, if any, you can import from the previous one.

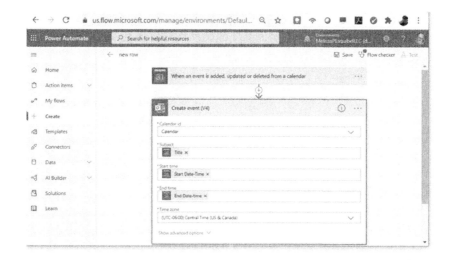

---

**Pro Tip: Word of Caution**

Collaborative tools essentially change your information management structure from 'push' (I will push information at you when it suits me via an email) to 'pull' (you choose what you see and at a time convenient to you). This is a very effective way to reduce information and email overload whilst simultaneously improving the quality of communications.

Maintain these benefits by receiving notifications at a rate that suits your workflow, not as a constant stream of alerts. Where possible, switch off app notifications and schedule time in your day to check notice boards. These tools can create a highly competitive environment as everyone competes to finish their tasks, post interesting information and add comments to a discussion. This can

---

either be good news or bad news, depending upon the challenges you are looking for these tools to address.

Used thoughtfully and with proper guidelines to solve a real business problem, these are powerful tools that will develop over time and may well replace internal email.

# CYBERSECURITY

# | Tip #66 |

## Cybersecurity

*Surveillance capitalism (is) a new hidden economic order that claims human experience as free raw material for hidden commercial practices of extraction, predication and sales.*
*- Shoshana Zuboff*

## The Challenge

During workshops we are often asked about ways, other than through email messages, that cyber criminals can hack your accounts to steal your identity and hence money. They are indeed many and varied. For example, in a café they can listen in to your keystrokes, pose as friends on social media and entice you to join a false wireless network. What are the ways that we must be alert, in addition to being aware of fake email (see 'Spot the fake email')?

## The Solution

*Situations Where You Unknowingly Disclose Information*

Here are 11 situations where you can fall victim to prying eyes and hence possibly a cyber-attack and the actions you can take to reduce the risk of leaving the door open for cyber-criminals.

1. Ordering any takeaway food where you give your name and wait in line for it to be made (for example, a coffee). The cyber criminals listen in and can quickly look you up, match image and start searching for information about you (where you work, hobbies and friends and family).

**Action** – Always look around at who is standing near you.

2. Outside the office, for example for lunch. Whether on your own or with friends, are you still wearing your organisation's ID in the form of a badge or lanyard which says where you work? Again, the door is open to the cyber criminals to find out more about you.

**Action** – Either remove or hide your work lanyard as soon as you leave the office (even if it's only to nip out for five minutes).

3. Out for exercise and using an app into which you feed your results like Fitbit, MyFitnessPal, or Strava. There have been several high-profile cases where cyber criminals have stolen personal data from these apps. The classic case is in the US, where highly sensitive personnel and sites were identified through Strava. Strava holds 1.3 terabytes of personal information, which is equivalent to about 400,000 copies of 'War & Peace'. Such app providers have improved their security and privacy options; nonetheless, over the last 18 months, Under Armour's MyFitnessPal had 150 million names, etc. hacked. PumpUp disclosed bio data with photos. Polar exposed sensitive data including geodata for secret agents and soldiers.

**Action** – Ask yourself: why are you uploading your data? Is it your competitive nature? If so, be aware of the trade-off between doing so and a possible cyber-attack. Maybe you can compete in other ways with friends rather than the whole world.

4. In a public place using your laptop or mobile device. Have you left the device open so that someone else can see the screen?

Do you realise that highly skilled cyber criminals have the equipment to listen to your keystrokes? Yes, each one makes a different sound which can be detected by the right equipment.

**Action** – First, always make sure you keep your devices close to you. When not in use, turn them face down, especially mobile ones such as phones and tablets (or close the holder in which they sit). Second, look around before you sit down to see if there is anyone who looks suspicious. If you feel in the least bit uncomfortable, either go elsewhere or sit as far as possible away from them.

5. Public Wi-Fi, for instance in a hotel, restaurant, coffee shop, museum, cinema or store. Even though you need a password to access them, they are still a very good back door for the cyber criminals who can clone them. The criminal can then access your keystrokes next time you log in automatically to that particular Wi-Fi.

**Action** – Always delete such networks from your saved list and relog in if you need to access them again. A pain, but once again, balance the inconvenience against being hacked and having your identity stolen. Alternatively, where possible use a VPN instead of a public website. You can buy a dongle which allows you to create your own VPN wherever you are.

6. Paying by credit card, especially in a public place (even with social distancing). When you go to pay, they use a decoy who stands far enough away, yet near enough to see you type in your pin. Often this is a child who just looks as though they are running around. (It happened to one of us; our wallet was then stolen, and the card used.) There is a school of thought that criminals can also skim your credit card details using an RFID (radio frequency identification device), but at the time of writing there is little evidence.

**Action** – As in Scenario 1, be alert to people near you even if they are socially distanced. If you are concerned about having your credit card details skimmed, keep them in an RFID blocking wallet.

7.  Social media accounts. People ask to be your Friend and join your network. There have been many instances when another person's identity has been cloned and the person making the request is in fact a cyber-criminals impersonating someone else.

**Action** – Check very carefully when you receive such requests. Any doubts, ignore the request.

8.  Conference calls. In the early days of the Covid 19 pandemic, it was not uncommon for cyber criminals to hack a Zoom call and ask to be admitted. Most video-conferencing systems have now added extra layers of security, but as the criminals up their game, no doubt they will find new ways to enter.

**Action** – Check that attendees are registered and if you have any concerns, refuse to admit them until you are sure. The obvious give away is a strange name. One of us did this for a board meeting only to discover the person was the previous late Chairman's wife who was using a pseudonym based on an African village she supported! The moral: don't use a pseudonym; use your proper name when registering for webinars etc.

9.  Fake website. Beware if you see a really good deal, better than anything you have already seen. We know one friend who nearly bought a car because it was $1,000 less than they had seen anywhere else. Warning bells started to ring, as the price was too good to be true. They researched again and saw the same vehicle on another site. The extra cheap one was a fake.

**Action** – Be suspicious of a deal too good to be missed. It is your money which will go missing. Keep searching and checking and, if need be, telephone the owner of the company before parting with money.

10. Social media in general. Over the last two years, on Facebook 40 million passwords have been stolen; on LinkedIn over one million credentials have been stolen.

Action – Be on your guard when you receive an unusual request and beware of how much personal information you post on all social media sites, especially data relating to recent purchases and holidays. Try to limit the use of your social media accounts to log on to other sites. Create new details and use a password manager to help you manage all the accounts – see Tip 44. Again, it takes time but minimises the risk of a cyber-attack.

11. Search engines – We all know they keep a certain amount of data.

Action – Consider using DuckDuckGo as an alternative to the usual search engines such as Google, Safari, Windows Explorer and Firefox. Not quite as efficient, but you have to make a choice of safety over being hacked. You can also improve how much information is retained and stay below the radar by auto deleting history as often as possible and manually clearing out any other old data such as cached pages. This means you have to re-enter your log in details, but it's a small price to pay.

12. Web-based advertisements. They popup all over the place and besides being annoying, they maybe fake. Ignore them.

**Action** – Make sure you use a good ad blocker such as Adblocker and antivirus software. Keep both up to date. The free versions will often be adequate for most users. However, if you are either a heavy user or run your own business, you will probably need a subscription-based version to provide better protection. If you are interested in the product being advertised, leave the original site on which you saw the advert and go to the advertiser's listed site.

## *Do we have any privacy in the 21st century?*

In a word, no. You need to be constantly on your guard. We now live in the world of constant surveillance, as described so admirably by

Shoshana Zuboff in her latest book. 'The Age of Surveillance Capitalism'. If it is not the cyber criminals capturing your personal data, it may be an organisation who will then sell it to another business! And we are talking reputable businesses for whom cross-selling data has now become a new revenue stream, despite all the laws surrounding the use of personal data.

If you have any doubts about how much information is stored and shared on the internet about you, go to the deep (and also dark) web to see what you can find (for example, through a browser like Tor). Or maybe not, if you do not want to be too depressed and stressed. Accept that this is the age we live in and be ultra-cautious about what you share and which sites you visit.

# ‖ Tip #67 ‖

## Out of Office Message – Overcome the Hidden Dangers

## The Challenge

I see all sorts of Out of Office messages, from short and simple saying when the person is on vacation to long and complex, even saying where they are going. Then there are those who say all their email messages are being deleted while they are away. Some people don't even use an OOO message because setting one can be a way to leak information to the prying eyes of, for example, as a cybercriminal.

What picture do these OOO messages convey of you and what is the cyber-security risk?

1. 'I am presently attending ABC Conference in Las Vegas with extremely limited access to email. I will not be returning to the UK until 02 October. If it is urgent…'

2. 'Bye guys and girls, I'm on honeymoon in Phuket and will not be back until 28 October. If your email is urgent…'

3. 'I am away from the office on annual leave until Monday 23 June 2008. Any queries, please contact Charlie Batty or Sophie Dingy on 22483/23429. Alternatively, you can contact one of the Strategic Development Managers as follows:

- Jacob Devine – E-learning via j.devine@org.com
- Michelle Hull – MBA Programme via m.hull@org.com
- David Day –– HR Planning via d.day@org.com'

## Your Image

What does your OOO message tell the recipient about you?

Example 1 – Are we paying your company (and you) too much to be spending time in Las Vegas?

Example 2 – Do we really need to know about your personal life and are you a show-off?

Example 3 – Look at how much information you have given away to prying eyes: five colleagues' names and their email addresses which hackers can now use. Chances are too that no one will read further than the first contact person and call them for whatever they need.

## The Cyber security Risks

In each case, too, you are shouting three things to the cyber-criminal. First, 'Come burgle my house', because it will not take them more than five minutes to find your address. Second, you are opening the door to some form of phishing attack (either spear or whaling). They will use your email address to impersonate you (or the named contact) and launch an email-born cyber-attack. Third, and worse still, they can use the information to pose as you to gain access to your offices. This is not uncommon during peak holiday time when the front desk is manned by different people.

## The Solution

What is best practice for setting your OOO message, both to save everyone time and reduce the potential security risk? The answer depends on two related factors. Firstly, any email you send is a picture of you, and that includes autoreplies like the OOO message.

Second, there may be a company policy to which you must adhere. If not, you must weigh up the security risks for yourself.

## OOO Content

It should contain the following two elements:

- Minimal information about why you are away from the office
- One emergency contact point – either a phone number or email address (preferably the former)

This is especially important as more people work from home. It protects you and your home.

Here is the ideal template:

'Thanks for your email. I am away from the office until X. If your email is urgent, please contact A on 01234 5678. Otherwise I will deal with it on my return.'

Now the cyber criminal does not know if you are away on business or if you are still at home or on leave. Are you in the building but in an all-day meeting?

### *Declaring vacation email bankruptcy*

This is getting more common: the OOO message tells you that the recipient is deleting all their received messages while out of the office and to re-send important ones after their return. It can be very effective, but you might need to be of a certain level of seniority and use it only with internal contacts.

### *Email buddy*

This is common amongst PAs and EAs: they check each other's mail when one of them is away. It negates the need for an OOO message and is thus the lowest security risk option.

## Different messages for internal and external contacts

You can have a different internal and external OOO message. For most situations, it is better to have a standard one like the template above.

However, you might want to consider setting your external OOO message for only those already in your contact list.

## The WFH option

Lastly, if you work for yourself from home, you should weigh up the security risk against the well-being factor in terms of not setting an OOO message and just checking your email a couple of times each day. The alternative is to find another person to monitor your inbox whilst you have a real digital detox!

## When to set the OOO

Here's an expert tip to improve your well-being. Set your OOO for a day before and a day after your return, thus giving yourself time to pack and unpack your inbox before anyone starts to nag you for a reply!

# Tip #68

## Spot the Fake Email

*Hackers attack (someone) every 39 seconds (and) on average 2,244 times a day.*
*–University of Maryland*

## The Challenge

Email remains the number one source (vector) for cyber-attacks: 94% of malware is delivered by email and phishing attacks account for 80% of all reported security breaches. During the Covid 19 pandemic there was a 600% growth in such malicious email attacks specifically focused on the pandemic.

The challenge for most of us is how to spot the fake email from the genuine one. To some extent, the more email messages you receive each day, the harder the challenge, as you fight your way through the daily tsunami which in many cases can be 100+ per day. Add to that a small screen if you are viewing your mail on a mobile device and you have added another barrier.

Moreover, the perpetrators, the cyber-criminals, are becoming cleverer by the day. They can expect to earn about £1.5m per year. Their attacks can be random to highly focused. They just need to catch one of us off guard.

## The Solution

These fake email messages come in several different forms and more often than not contain some easy to spot warning signs as outlined below. The most robust defence to email message born cyber attacks is to be alert. If you have the slightest doubt about the authenticity of the email, phone the sender to check if it really was from them.

## The Different Types of Fake Email Messages

Malicious (or, as we call them, fake) messages come in about five major forms. The first step is to recognise what you are dealing with.

1.  Spam containing malware. This can be in the form of a link to a bogus website, attachments or software to log your key strokes. The sender is generally either trying to obtain your account information or drop a virus on your device and extract money to remove it. Below is a typical example.

2.  Ransom demand for money. They will say they have your passwords, indicate you have visited some inappropriate website or say, they are stranded and need money. In the case of passwords, they have often obtained your email address and password from a website which was hacked some time ago, e.g. LinkedIn, Booking.com, Marriot, Facebook, etc. The cyber criminals hold on to the addresses for a while on the assumption you will have forgotten about the hack.

3.  Phishing. Addresses are generated randomly in a scatter-gun approach and look as though they are from trusted friends or organisations. Again, the hacker is looking to access your login details.

4.  Spear phishing. A more refined form of phishing is based on a specific thing you like, e.g. wine, jewellery or restaurants. This is data gleaned from your social media profiles and internet footprint. The message will be tailored to your taste. Sometimes the criminal will have

hacked the other person's website. This is typical where there is a money transfer involved, for example to a solicitor.

5. Whaling. An even more refined and harder to spot form of spear phishing. Here the person, often a top executive, has had their email address hacked. The attacker sends email messages on issues of critical business importance, masquerading as an individual or organisation with legitimate authority. For example, an attacker may send an email to a CFO requesting payment, pretending to be a client of the company. A typical example is shown below.

```
From: ▓▓▓▓▓▓▓▓▓▓▓▓▓▓▓▓
Sent: 31 October 2019 12:59
To: ▓▓▓▓▓▓▓▓▓▓▓▓▓▓▓▓▓▓▓>
Subject:


--
Are you free at the moment ?

Regards.
```

```
From: ▓▓▓▓▓▓▓▓▓▓▓▓▓▓▓▓
Sent: 31 October 2019 13:09
To: ▓▓▓▓▓▓▓▓▓▓▓▓▓▓▓▓▓▓▓
Subject: Re: Free

I'm having a private meeting with the AMAZON corporation about a proposed school project and I need you to help
me purchase AMAZON gift cards from a nearest shop needed urgently at the meeting and send me pictures of it over
the email. I will reimburse you once I'm done with the meeting. I will appreciate if you can do this right away
and communicate with me via email. Because I can not make use of phones during meeting. Thanks
```

## *Key warning signals*

While the cybercriminals are upping their game, they rely on machines. No matter what form of fake, these are the top 10 clues that indicate that the message is not genuine.

1. The address. It might look like the email address of someone you know, even the CEO, but on careful inspection it is different. Typically, if it is from an organisation it will contain a public domain name - for example, j.smith@gmail instead of j.smith@executiverecruitemt.com. Alternatively, if it is from someone with a public domain address, the address will look

unusual, what is normally monica@gmail.com might be mon1ca@gmail.com

2. Spelling mistakes. These are very common.

3. Use of capitals in the middle of a word or sentence. Again, common.

4. Unusual salutation. For example, 'Hiya' when the sender would normally just say 'Hi', use your name, etc.

5. Subject line. Often conveys a sense of urgency - for example, 'Are you free now'; 'Read this it's important'; 'Urgent transfer of funds needed'; 'Your licence will be suspended in three days time'; 'Be sure to read this as you data has been compromised'; 'Act now'.

6. Using the word 'login' instead of log in'. This is subtle. 'Login' is a noun and refers to the details you use to access your account, e.g. username/password, whereas 'log in' is a verb used to describe the process/action taken to access your account, i.e. to type in your login details! The hackers often make this mistake and use the noun and ask you to 'please login to your account' instead of 'please log in to your account'.

7. Link to strange websites.

8. Green padlock beside the website. A green padlock simply indicates that the website has an SSL certificate, which means that data shared between your device and the website is encrypted. It does not mean it is a genuine website.

9. Being asked to provide additional personal data. The hackers assume that now that you have logged into their fake website, you will not mind giving away more personal data, e.g. the name of your pet, best friend etc.

10. Unusual/strange attachments when none were expected. For example, it might be from a genuine address but say something like 'you must read this new report'.

The most robust defence to any type of malicious email message is to be alert to these warning signals and phone the recipient before acting on the email and its content.

# Tip #69

## Create Strong Passwords to Reduce the Risk of a Cyber attack

## The Challenge

A strong password is one of the most important ways to deter cyber criminals. Did you know that these are the 10 most frequently used passwords?

- 123456
- 123456789
- 12345678
- 1234567
- qwerty
- password
- 12345
- 111111
- sunshine
- iloveyou

They are weak and easily guessed by even the most inexperienced cybercriminal! And of course, then you have your partner's pet', parent's name, or the last place you visited on holiday. Again, a cybercriminal can easily guess these by doing a little homework on social media.

## The Solution

## How Do You Create Strong Passwords Which You Can Remember?

A strong password should be at least eight characters and contain upper and lower case letters, some numbers and at least one special character (!, *, +, @ and so on.). The longer and more complex the password, the better. Twenty characters is the recommendation for real strength.

The simplest way is to create a sentence which means something to you and use the first letter of each word and add in a mix of the above. Here is an example

I am writing this new book with Jane for book publishing. Converted to a password, it might be:

1 @WtnBwJ4bP

How strong is this password? Very, when checked by LastPass (see https://lastpass.com/howsecure.php).

It would take 400 years for someone to crack – as measured by one online password security checker, 'Howsecureismypassword' (see https://howsecureismypassword.net/).

Indeed, many websites will tell you how strong your password is as you create it.

## Can You Use Just This One Password For Everything?

No. Ideally, you need a separate one for each site. In addition to the sentence method, you might take a name and similarly convert it to a mix of upper and lower case letters, numbers and special symbols. For example:

Samantha Brown might become 3@ManTh@Br0wn. This is rated as 'very strong' 'and would potentially take three million years to crack.

## How Do I Remember All These Different Passwords?

That is a real challenge. One option is to use one of the specialist password management apps (see 'Password Management Apps'). Never write down your passwords or store them in any electronic file.

# | Tip #70 |

## Password Management Apps

## The Challenge

'I have so many passwords it's hard to remember them all. I try not to reuse the same one, but creating a new strong one for each site can be hard. Also, some need changing every so often. I heard that password management apps are a good way to manage secure passwords. Are they worth it? How do they work, and which are the best ones?'

## The Solution

A recent Microsoft study revealed that most of us have about seven different passwords which we use across about 25 different sites. During the height of the Covid 19 pandemic, there was a significant rise in the number of passwords which were stolen mainly through malicious email messages (phishing attacks).

## Pros of Password Management Apps

There are five main factors in favour of using such apps.

1. They provide increased security and reduce the risk of having your passwords and hence personal identity stolen.

Strong passwords should be at least 8 characters with 20 as the recommended norm. This can be hard to type on a mobile device.

2. The password manager takes care of this aspect as it automatically recalls and inserts the password.

3. The app overcomes the danger associated with using the same password for each site, as it generates a different one for each site.

4. It alerts you if either your account or a site you use has been hacked.

5. It allows you to share a password securely with another trusted person (who will not be able to see the characters).

## Cons of Password Management Apps

There are five central arguments for not using such apps.

1. It is a single point for the hacker to access all your passwords, and there have been some high-profile attacks. However, most apps now encrypt your data to reduce this risk.

2. They do not all synchronise across all devices and therefore you have to install the app on each device.

3. If you lose your master password and/or key identity data, you may lose all your passwords.

4. They do not all work with all browsers, although that is becoming less of a concern.

5. Although many offer a free version, most have a subscription fee.

Overall, the pros of enhanced security outweigh the cons, first and most importantly in terms of the cost (financial and emotional) of being hacked. Second, there is a wide choice of apps from which to choose to meet your needs, as discussed below.

## Key Criteria in Choosing a Password Management App

Before looking at the different apps, it is crucial to decide what you need, rather like moving to a new house or buying a new car. Below is a list of 14 important features which you might need.

1. Two-factor authentication (2FA). After entering your password, you will be asked to enter a second piece of data, typically provide biometric identification such as a fingerprint, answer a question to which only you know the answer or type in a code sent to an alternative device/email address. Takes an extra few seconds, but weigh this up against the cost of having your identity stolen.

2. Ease of use. As a rule of thumb, the more sophisticated, the more difficult the software is to use until you really understand it. Some apps have some deeply technical functions which the average user will not need.

3. Encrypts the saved passwords. This means that even if the hacker did obtain access to your device and your master password, they would not be able to access the passwords held within the password management app.

4. Cross-platform compatibility and synchronisation. If you have a Windows desktop/laptop and an iOS mobile device (e.g. iPad) make sure the app can be used across all platforms and synchronises across them.

5. Works on your favourite browser. Most work on Google Chrome, Safari, and Mozilla Firefox but not all work on, for instance, Opera.

6. Flags duplicate and weak passwords.

7. Automatically generates strong passwords if needed.

8. Rates the strength of those you create yourself.

9. Captures and replays passwords and key credentials.

10. Auto form filling, although some would say this is to be avoided. However, it is helpful and saves you time (and the chance of making an error) when re-typing the same data each time.

11. Can manage multiple logins to the same site and offer you a choice as to which one you want to use.
12. Secure document storage. It does not replace the need for either a cloud or specialist back-up service but allows you space to store encrypted files. Useful for storing important documents like copy of passport, driving licence.
13. Share a password with another user but without them seeing the actual password. Useful if you are someone who takes 'digital legacy' seriously and hence how others access your web-based accounts (from financial to social media) on either death or if you are seriously incapacitated.
14. Allows you to export/import your data if you change apps.

Once you have decided your priorities, there is the cost. Some offer a free version of the app with limited features and some are only available on subscription.

## Password Management Apps

Of the available apps, it's hard to prioritise one over the other because what is number one today might have changed even by the time this book is published simply because they all play catch-up. New features on one soon become available on others. At the time of writing this book, the five most popular are LastPass, Dashlane, 1Password, Bitwarden and Keeper.

- LastPass is easy to use and offers a free version which has all the basic security functions, although currently it does not alert you to security breaches.
- Dashlane includes security alerts and scanning the Dark Web for compromised accounts.
- 1-Password is thought to be the best for multiple users.
- Bitwarden has a very sophisticated two-factor authentication and appeals to those more technically minded.

- Keeper is rated for those for whom encrypted file-sharing is critical.

Others to consider are:

- Zoho Vault
- RoboForm
- LogMeOnce
- NordPass
- PassBoss
- Sticky Password Premium
- True Key
- mSecure

## It's Your Choice

At the end of the day, it is about which of the key criteria are important to you and, when two apps are similar, the cost. Lastly, if you decide to trial the free version of one of these apps (always a good idea), check that you can export, then import the data to another one. Otherwise, you will have to manually re-enter it all again!

# | Tip #71 |

## Top Tips to Avoid an Email Disaster

## The Challenge

'Last week, in haste, a client replied to an email and within minutes an email war had broken out. The recipient felt the content contained words which indicated a level of prejudice. Nothing could have been further from their mind. It took a few days for the storm to blow over-time which could have been better spent on other high priority business matters. All very stressful too. This is not the first time something like this has happened within my organisation. How can we reduce the risk of inadvertently causing such email disasters?'

## The Solution

We often hear reports of an 'emailgate' disaster where someone has written, replied to or leaked an email which causes offence and, in some cases, untold damage to their public person or the reputation of their organisation. Think Hillary Clinton's campaign boss, John Podesta and David Beckham, both of whose email was leaked. The term 'emailgate' comes from the issues surrounding Clinton's use of a personal email server rather than a government secured one, and the Podesta email leaks are believed to have contributed to her losing the US presidential election in 2016. In 2017, Beckham complained about his lack of a Knighthood (which at the time of writing he still does not have).

Remember, too, that how you write email is your 'digital dress code'; it is how people judge you, especially if they have never met you (either face-to-face or via a conference call).

Here are our top 10 ways to reduce the risk of starting an emailgate type disaster.

1. Pause before hitting Send and ask yourself what will be the consequence if this email is taken out of context? If this email were forwarded, is the content something that I want other people to know about?

2. Never send email messages if you are under the influence of alcohol.

3. Never email when you are feeling angry or overly emotional.

4. Check and re-check that you are sending the email to the right person: Frank Smith and not Frank Smithers, Jane Wise and not Jane Williams. Type-ahead tips are great, but they can lead you to a very costly mistake.

5. If the content is either sensitive or might be deemed emotional, always talk first.

6. If someone sends you an email which you feel is out of order (for example, they are angry or are criticising you or your work), wait at least two hours before replying. When you reply, defuse the anger by being as objective as possible. Alternatively, talk to the sender before replying by email.

7. Check your own email messages to ensure that none of your words can be misinterpreted. For example, the simple word 'thanks' can mean many different things, from genuine gratitude to 'thanks for dropping me in it'.

8. Avoid sending jokes and using emoticons on your business email account because they can easily be misinterpreted

9. Be sensitive to gender issues, titles and people's names. (See 'Signature Line Etiquette'.)

10. Write a rule which sends all your email to the draft box before they actually leave your device. This gives you time to re-read your email before it goes.

## How to Delay Sending Email

There are several ways to do this. First, here is how to write a rule to delay sending an email by say three minutes.

1. Go to Rule/Manage Rules & Alerts

2. From the Rules and Alerts dialogue box, click on the New Rule tab

3. Pick 'Apply rule on messages I send' (bottom option). Click Next.

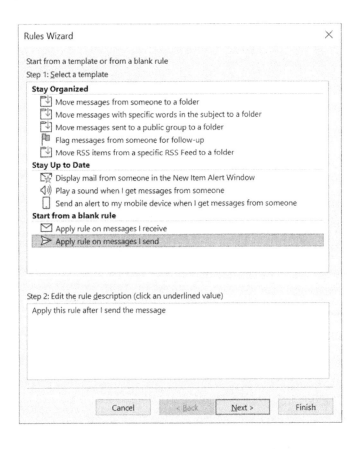

4.  Select 'through this account'. You are then prompted to fill in your email account (Step 2). Click Next.

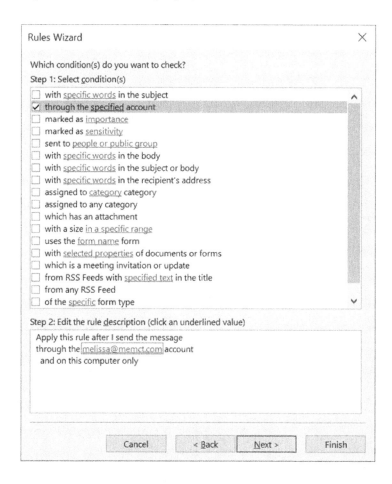

5.  Pick 'defer delivery by a number of minutes'. Click on 'number of minutes' (Step 2 box below) and choose the delay time, e.g. three minutes. Click OK. Click Next.

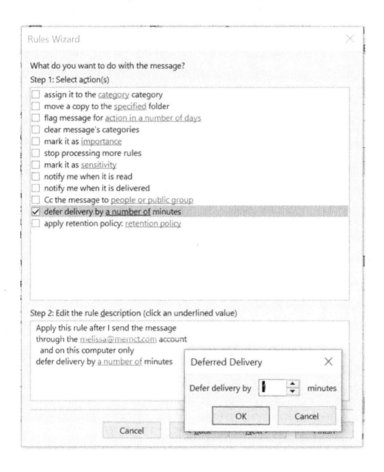

6. You are now offered some exceptions, e.g. to certain people. Bypass these by clicking Finish.

Now every email you send will sit in your draft box for three minutes before it is sent. This can be a real time saver, not only in terms of avoiding a disaster but also reducing unnecessary rounds of email ping-pong in case you have not included all the data the recipient might need before proceeding.

## Quick Steps

You can also create a Quick Step that delays delivery by one minute automatically. (See 'Save Time Sending the Same Content with Quick Steps').

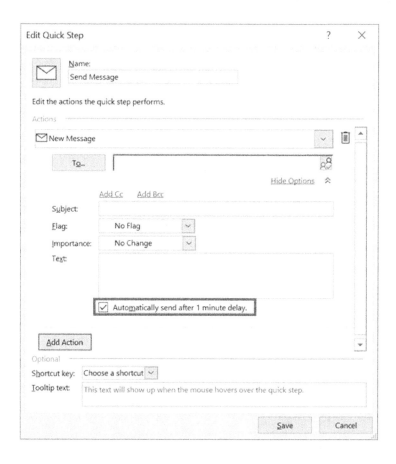

## Gmail Users

Use the Schedule function. Click on the up arrow beside the Send button.

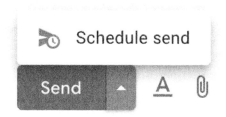

Now pick when you send the email from the Schedule dialogue box.

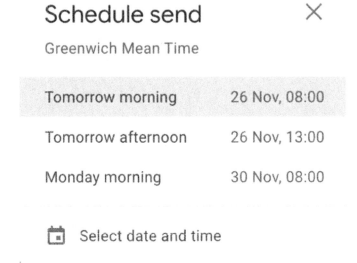

If you change your mind and want to send the email sooner, open the email now saved in the Scheduled folder and click on 'Cancel send'.

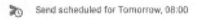

## Bad Email Always Turns Up Like Bad Pennies

Still not convinced of the need to slow down and pause before hitting Send? Remember, there is no such thing as 'recalling' an email because even if it was sent back, the chances are the recipient read it before it was returned. Someone somewhere will have saved that email, and it will turn up when you least expect it. (See 'Recalling Messages: The Hard Truth.')

# CALENDARS AND DIARIES

# Tip #72

## Meeting-Free Time to Reduce Email Overload

### The Challenge

Philippa (my boss) spends at least 85% of her days in meetings (either face-to-face or virtual). This means the email mounts up during the daytime. Even with me managing her inbox, she often has to spend time well outside normal working hours clearing the back log (sometimes even weekends).

'I recently audited my own and Philippa's inbox and found that many of the messages are from her team and are either requesting a meeting with her or long chains (conversations) which could easily (and more quickly) be resolved with an actual conversation. What can I do to help reduce the volume of these types of email messages in both our inboxes (because I am often copied in as her team, I feel I can help in some way?'

### The Solution

This is a very common scenario and it's not surprising you are both suffering from chronic email overload. There is not much free time in Philippa's day for either 'me' time (for her to deal with her own work) or for colleagues to pop in for informal meetings. So, they have to resort to email.

The solution is easy: keep slots in her diary clear either every day or at least twice a week. You do not necessarily need to mark the time as busy; just keep it clear and don't accept meeting requests for these times. If you operate an open calendar then mark the slots as something like 'Team Time' or 'Thinking Time' and set it as private. Let the team know that this is when she is in her office and that they are free to drop in and see her with their questions, etc.

Clients who adopt this approach often see the email traffic drop by at least 20% because colleagues know that the non-urgent stuff can wait until they can talk to the boss.

Clearly there will be days when you have to release this protected time, but you will be amazed at the difference it makes and how often a meeting can be scheduled for a different time.

# ‖ Tip #73 ‖

## The Myth of 'Back-to-Back' Meetings

Top of the hour, bottom of the hour, 30 minutes, 1 hour are all convenient boundaries in which to fit a seemingly endless quantity of meetings. But should your next meeting begin directly after the previous one ends? Scheduling too tightly really doesn't help you get more done; it actually robs each session of its full productivity potential as people show up late, inadequately prepared and stressed out. It is, however, a well-accepted practice.

## The Challenge

Here are some questions to ask before giving away every moment of the workday.

1. If the meeting requires physical attendance or presence in a specific location, how long will it take to get from one place to the next?

    a) If everyone is in the office environment, how likely is it that you will be waylaid by impromptu social chats or 'got a second?' questions?

    b) If driving to another location, what is traffic like at that point in the day? Is parking close to the building? What changes if the weather is bad?

2.  How much preparation is required to meaningfully participate in the meeting? Keep in mind that a 'once over' review two days prior may not be enough to truly prepare you.

    a)  If meeting times are short and/or people are often late, wasting an additional 15 minutes telling everyone why they are there and what is expected of them is adding insult to injury. If you did not schedule adequate time to prepare, that's on you.

    b)  Is it possible that information has been updated right up till the meeting time? If it's your meeting, do you expect that people have had time to see the updates?

3.  If the meeting is online only, how much time will be required for people to sign on and deal with audio/video/internet bandwidth issues before the meeting can start? If meetings aren't back-to-back, then the expectation is that the time to connect is 15 minutes prior to start.

4.  How effective are your meetings in general? Meeting duration should be a fair estimate of how much time it will take given the participants, the level of preparation required to attend and the agenda. If you're not sure, keep doing what you're doing and assess how meeting time unfolds.

    a)  What happens at the beginning and end of the meeting?
    b)  Did you get to all the agenda items?
    c)  Was there time for a proper wrap up?
    d)  Were there items for which no one was prepared? Did you need to schedule additional meetings to wrap things up?
    e)  Did everyone contribute or were there people who did not need to be there?
    f)  Did the meeting break early or go over time?
    g)  Were people considerate meeting participants or were they talking over each other and interrupting?

# The Solution

Even implementing one or two of these can buy some significant productivity back for your organisation.

1. First of all, there's no law that says meetings must start and end on the hour or half hour. Feel free to start them at 10:10 a.m. or 3:42 p.m. Actually, if you start them at an odd time, people may be more likely to be on time.

2. Allot only the estimated time it takes to get things done. So, if the meeting objectives can be met in 45 minutes, don't schedule an hour. If the meeting can be effectively concluded in 20 minutes, consider stand-up meetings. Start at 10 minutes after the hour for example, with a commitment to leave at the bottom of the hour.

3. Could you be taking advantage of other means of collaboration? Does this even need to be a meeting? Can we start a Teams Channel or Google Jamboard with each member participating at their convenience, but by a deadline with a final review time period so everyone can see everyone's contributions or ideas? If the meeting is really an address by one person to a group, can that person record a video post it to your collaboration platform and initiate an online Q&A chat or discussion board for questions?

4. In your calendaring program, be it Outlook, Google Calendar or something else, when you receive a meeting invitation, decline it if you cannot schedule at least 15-30 minutes ahead of it to adequately prepare and additional time if you need to move from one place to the next. If you can, then add an appointment (not a meeting) and mark the time as Busy for the amount of prep/travel time you'll need.

5. Use a category without a colour to keep your prep/travel time from cluttering your calendar and making scheduled meeting time too difficult to see. If you prepare conference rooms for

meetings, use this same technique to set aside time to make sure the room is ready to go when the participants are.

6. Utilise reminders to notify you the day before for meetings that require a great deal of preparation, a week before if catering will be needed and eight weeks before if travel (beyond a car trip across town) is required.

7. Evangelise! Schedule a lunch to learn with those who schedule meetings and talk about new ground rules.

8. When viewing someone's calendar, do not schedule meetings directly after the previous meeting on the calendar.

9. Everyone is expected to show up to meetings prepared, allowing additional time for travel and/or connection to online meeting portals.

10. Meeting etiquette will be enforced. No talking over each other, show up on time, stay on track and on topic.

# Tip #74

## The Meeting Before the Meeting

## The Challenge

In a world where people are still scheduling back-to-back meetings, it's hard to wedge in the preparation that needs to happen in order for meetings to be successful and efficient. Consider the current times of many video conferences. So much time gets wasted with getting connected, getting people to mute their microphones, sending meeting materials in chat and dealing with last-minute stragglers.

## The Solution

Before every meeting, start scheduling a Meeting Before the Meeting (MBTM). Depending upon the size and complexity of the meeting, this might be 15 minutes or as much as 30 minutes, even an hour! If your meeting is occurring in physical space, try to reserve the room for your meeting that much time ahead of the actual start. Block this time on your calendar as you would any other appointment to be sure you can take full advantage of the time.

Here are the activities to consider for your MBTM.

- Access the video conference portal or meeting room to make sure everything is operating correctly.

- If you're in a physical room, be sure that room is sufficiently cleaned and disinfected before you guests arrive. This may also mean coordinating this activity with maintenance staff who are specially trained in hygiene protocols.
- If you have ordered food for your meeting, have it arrive during your MBTM, if at all possible. In this way, no interruptions will delay the smooth conduct of the proceedings.
- If packets need to be distributed or attachments added to the meeting portal, this would be the time to ensure those are in place.
- Inform attendees to a video conference that they should connect 10 minutes prior to the actual meeting start. You could also just schedule the meeting to begin at 10 minutes before the hour if you think people will be likely to ignore your efforts to have the meeting begin on time.
- If you have any time left in your MBTM allotment, use it to review the agenda, order of presenters and any potential hiccups you might need to address.

Now, rather than being frazzled trying to do everything at the last minute, you're calm, your meeting participants are in attendance and you can deal with anything you didn't think of. (See 'The Myth of 'Back-to-Back" Meetings')

# ‖ Tip #75 ‖

## Managing Multiple Calendars in Outlook

## The Challenge

Most administrative professionals are supporting more than one person. Even with the best tools in the world, this can be challenging. The best advice here is non-technical: establish ground rules with those whom you support. Here's a list to get you started.

1. Who may and may not add items to your calendar?
2. Who may and may not delete items from or move items onto your calendar?
3. Who will send, accept and decline meeting requests?

## The Solution

While different executives prefer to maintain different levels of control over their time allotments, there are several ways you can work in Outlook to make the task of juggling calendars easier.

## Views

You may view several calendars at the same time by simply checking individuals' calendars on the left in the navigation pane.

Up to four calendars will reveal themselves in quadrants. Beyond that, you will see them stacked, one on top of the other. If you have multiple time zones shown, you will see those at the top now, rather than on the left as you would in Day, Week or Work Week view.

An alternative to this if you are working with multiple monitors is to right-click on a calendar name and choose Open in New Window. In this manner, and depending upon the size of your monitors, you could have many calendars open in a 'non-stacked' view and be able to see things clearly. A couple of things to help in these views is to collapse the navigation pane (left) and minimise the ribbon. Notice that the ribbon will either be minimised on all windows or none of them. However, the navigation pane can be manipulated independently.

No matter which one you choose, use the Colour option to vary the colours on each calendar. If you're consistent with this across other things like Categories as they pertain to the people you support, your eyes become accustomed to focusing on the particular calendars and items you need.

## Categories

Put 10 people in a room who use Outlook categories and you may come up with just that many ways to use them. Here are the basics of how to create and apply colour categories.

1. Right click any Outlook item, such as an appointment, and choose Categorize. If you see a listing such as Red Category, Blue Category, Green Category, look to the bottom of the fly-out menu for All Categories.
2. Here, you may either rename an existing category or create a new one by clicking the New button.
3. After clicking the New button, you will assign it a name and a colour. There are 25 colours to choose from and they may be applied to more than one category name. You may also choose no colour at all.

One way to use the no colour choice is to assign a category to 'meeting before the meeting' time. That means the time you use to go in and set up the meeting room or meeting portal and get everything printed or sent to everyone. On your calendar, you could assign the colour of one of your executives to the actual meeting, and the time before it no colour for your set-up time. That way, your time is allotted but doesn't visually interfere with the actual meetings on the calendar (that is, if you choose to make your categories match the people you support). Other applications are:

- By client
- By type of meeting (one-on-one, committee, online, in person, offsite, etc.)
- By priority (must attend, should attend, optional)

## Permissions

One thing that has always been frustrating for administrative professionals is that colour categories are only applicable and visible on their own calendars unless they have Editor or Owner level of access (preferably Owner) for an executive's calendar. Right-click a calendar and choose Properties to determine what level of access you've been granted.

This leads us back to the first topic, ground rules. If you have been challenged by an executive that insists on managing his or her own calendar, leaving you to mop up the mess created by conflicting appointments and others' priorities, this challenge can be met by gradually building trust and helping them understand that their time is too valuable to spend on managing a calendar, which is what you are an expert on!

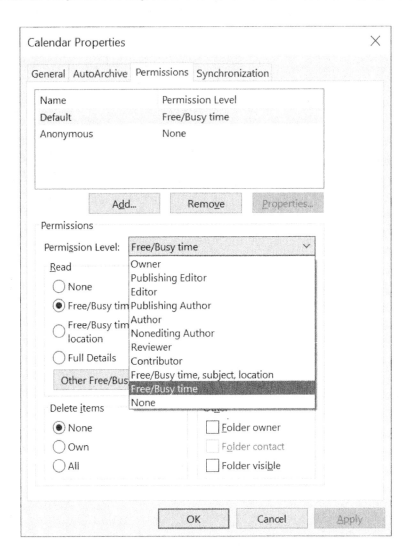

# Tip #76

## Managing Multiple Calendars in Google Workspace

### The Challenge

Though Google Calendar appears to be more streamlined and less cluttered, it is not as stripped down and lacking in features as you might think! Managing the calendars of multiple executives is always a challenge, regardless of the technology platform being used. In order to do your job effectively, you will need access to your executives' calendars to the level that allows you to create, move and delete events as priorities and schedules change. For new executives or those who have never had administrative support before, it may seem like a tug-of-war at first. Once trust is established, however, they'll wonder why they ever managed their own calendar.

### The Solution

### Sharing Calendars

Each person whose calendar you'll be managing will need to share their calendar with you. To do that, they'll follow these steps.

1.  Click the settings gear in the upper right corner of the Calendar screen.

2.  Locate the desired calendar under 'Settings for my calendars' and click it.

3.  Scroll down to see the 'Share with specific people' section.

4.  Click '+ Add people' and have them add you on the next dialogue.

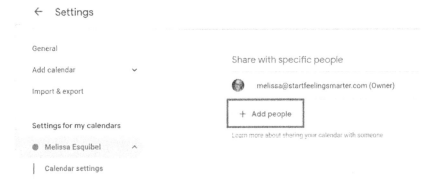

5.  In the second field in that dialogue, they can grant the appropriate permission level. (Make changes and manage sharing is recommended for those that are expected to manage another's calendar.)

6.  Click Send.

7. You will receive an email in your Gmail inbox indicating that they have shared a calendar with you.

8. Open the email message and click the link to 'Add this calendar.'

9. You will need to confirm it on the dialogue that follows, as well.

10. Now you will see it under the My Calendars section.

In all but Day view the items will be colour-coded by calendar name. In Day view, you will be able to see the calendars side by side.

## Agenda Mode

One way to see how your day is shaping up, as well as the days of those you support, is to use Schedule view. To see your daily schedule on the screen, from the View selector, choose Schedule. Each calendar will have its own colour-coded dot next to the calendar event.

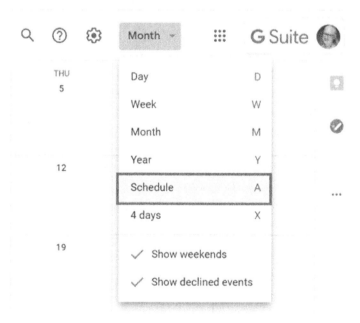

Show your executives this view. In fact, they can get their daily schedule emailed to them wherever they are so they can see any changes you may have made. Here are the steps they will follow.

1. In their calendar, click the settings gear in the upper right corner of the Calendar screen.

2. Select the calendar on the left.

3. Scroll to 'Other notifications'.

4. Locate 'Daily agenda' and toggle None to Email.

Keeping them updated in this way will inspire confidence in your calendar management abilities.

# ‖ Tip #77 ‖

## Sharing Your Calendar Information in Outlook

## The Challenge

Dealing with a barrage of phone calls and email messages about calendar availability is a timewaster. By default, all Outlook profiles are established to share Free/Busy information across the organisation. While this can be turned off, either by the organisation or the individual, it is not recommended. When someone tries to schedule a meeting, they will only know that you are either available or unavailable. It might be better to share more information about your calendar items with certain individuals, such as the people you support, as well as your admin colleagues.

## The Solution

Internal Company Calendar Sharing

You can share your calendar by using the following procedure.

1. Navigate to your calendar and click the Share Calendar icon in the ribbon. You can also right-click your calendar and click the Share option, then Share Calendar.

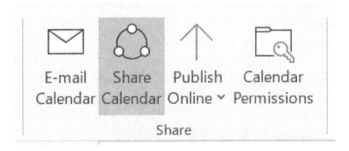

2. This creates an email message which you will address to the person with whom you'd like to share your calendar. You can, at the same time, request permission to view their calendar by checking the box.

3. Set the permission level you wish to grant them: Availability only, Limited details or Full details. Limited details will show the subject and location for meetings and appointments not marked private. Full details will show all details of meetings and appointments not marked private.

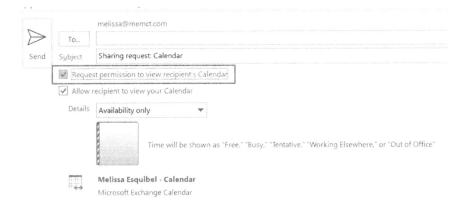

4. Click Send.

They will receive an email with a link to add your calendar to their Shared Calendar section. If they confirm sharing with you, you will receive the same type of email to add theirs.

## External Sharing

If you are trying to set up a meeting with individuals outside your organisation, it might be best to just send them your availability. You can start this process in three different ways.

- From the Calendar window, click the Email Calendar button just to the left of the Share Calendar button.

- Right-click the calendar in the navigation pane on the left and choose Share, then Email Calendar from the fly-out menu.

- From an email message you are composing, on the Insert tab, choose Calendar.

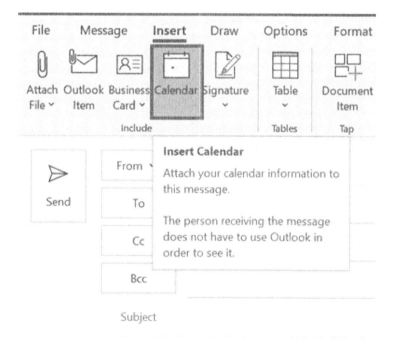

There are several options for what to share, which can be selected from the next dialogue. You can choose the date range to include and the level of details to share. This option does not provide direct access to your calendar, just the information on it so others can determine best times to schedule with you.

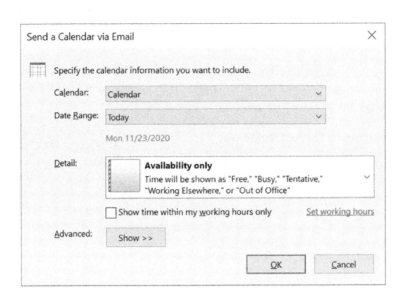

# ‖ Tip #78 ‖

## Using Outlook Calendar Scheduling Tools

### The Challenge

Finding time for people to meet is one of the most challenging tasks for many administrative professionals. Microsoft Outlook has two tools built in that can help you meet this challenge.

### The Solution

### Scheduling Assistant

The Scheduling Assistant has moved around some in Outlook over recent versions. In the most recent version, as of this writing, it is a ribbon tab in the desktop version and a toolbar button in Outlook Online. They work similarly by presenting you with a timeline grid. For individuals with whom you share calendar information, their availability will be shown to you so you can visually determine when they are available. The more individuals and calendar information shared, the more complex the display may be. You can use the AutoPick button (previously located at the bottom of the window) to automatically find times that work for everyone.

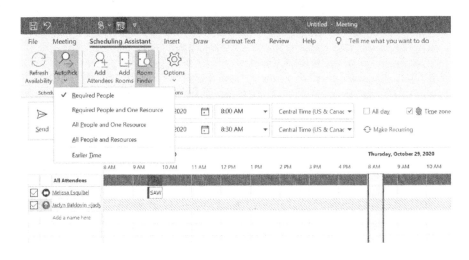

The quality of the information presented is dependent on how generously information is shared and the workday settings for each person. This can become trickier as meeting attendees span time zones. The timeline presented at the top of the display will always be yours. If you are the one scheduling multi-time zone meetings, it may help to expand your workday. Do this by going to Files, Options, Calendar (Windows) or Preferences, Calendar (Mac). Set the time span to include the earliest and latest worktimes for people with whom you may be scheduling time.

The non-tech part of this equation may be a little more challenging. By default, Exchange sets up calendar sharing to default as Free/Busy. This means that, while you won't see any meeting details, you will see whether someone has that time blocked. For those whom you support, it is recommended that you see at least limited details, though full details may be even more useful. If you need to schedule a meeting which may conflict with another appointment, if that appointment isn't as critical, it may make the task easier to accomplish. Of course, in this case, there would be some agreement in place regarding which appointments or events can be scheduled over and which cannot.

If your organisation in general, or even select individuals are a bit stingy with sharing their free/busy information, one way to effect change is to track how long it takes you to schedule meetings without it. Share this with them or those who can influence their decisions.

Often, people are not aware of the downline effect of playing their calendar cards so close to the vest.

## Room Finder

These days, by default if you activate the Scheduling Assistant in Outlook Desktop, you will also see the Room Finder at the right. Sometimes the hardest part of getting people together isn't their availability but finding a place to meet. As well, if specialised equipment must also be scheduled, the problem gets more complicated. The Room Finder uses a colour shading system to show you Good, Fair and Poor chances of finding meeting rooms. When you choose a date, it will list available rooms and resources in the box below the calendar display. You can choose it from here to add it to your meeting and reserve it.

While this tool does, as advertised, help you locate conference rooms or meeting resources which have been properly entered by the Exchange administrator, it can also help you determine meeting times. After including everyone on the invitee list and selecting an available conference room and any additional resources, you will see a list of suggested times below which indicates the potential number of calendar conflicts.

If you prefer not to work with Room Finder, you may click the Room Finder button to the right of the Location field in the main area of the invitation. If you change your mind, you can click it again to turn it on.

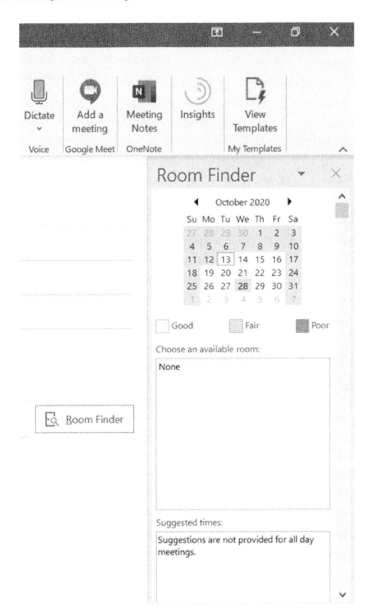

# | Tip #79 |

## The Recurring Meeting: Friend or Foe?

Getting time on people's calendars can be an uphill battle. One way to deal with it is to create recurring meetings for extended periods of time, even if the meeting may not actually happen. When enough people practice this method, however, meetings, appointments and events end up being booked in conflict with other reserved time. The fallout is that organisations find it difficult to stay nimble and react to the unexpected. At no time more frequently than the present day, the unexpected seems to occur frequently.

## The Challenge

There are two challenges. The first is, as discussed, reserving time which may or may not be used just in case, in effect holding others' time 'hostage.' The other is more practical. Creating the same meeting over and over seems an unnecessary replication of effort given that our calendar management tools give us the recurring meeting function. The first issue has the tendency to snowball and create choked calendars and no room to react to new priorities and projects.

## The Solution

This originally began back in the day when the only way to truly, actively collaborate was face-to-face.

For many in management, it is a control issue. Only when they see everyone on their team sitting in front of them do they believe they have their attention. The practice of taking time hostage really does nothing to improve this undesirable phenomenon. There are so many ways that we can collaborate now; 'regular' meetings should be revisited to evaluate whether they are the best use of staff time. Nothing in this chapter will address that problem in particular. However, see 'Are You a Technology Leader or Follower?' for tips on how to champion the use of new tools.

To reduce the repetitive task of setting up a recurring meeting, here are several methods to consider.

- Limit the time to which recurring meetings may be extended. For example, work on getting colleagues to agree that three or six months is the farthest out recurring meetings can be extended. Then, on the final message in the series, add an agenda item to determine whether the meeting should be continued.

- Don't set up any recurring meetings! Instead, use a Quick Step to set up a template for a meeting which may be repeated. On the Quick Steps drop-down (More button), choose New Meeting. Click the Options button to bring up a more detailed dialogue. Then, click on Show Options to compose all the fields necessary to create a meeting request. You can preset attendees, subject, location and even the agenda in the Text field. When it's time to set up a meeting, click the Quick Step, adjust the body and send it.

- Determine what justification there should be for a meeting by asking these questions:

  - Can the information to be imparted in the meeting be effectively imparted in an email message?

  - Should there be some collaboration in another platform first to ensure that the time spent in the meeting is minimal?

  - Do attendees have at least an 80% chance of sharing thoughts, ideas and feedback in the meeting?

You may find (and help your colleagues discover) that many of the meetings scheduled aren't even necessary.

# ‖ Tip #80 ‖

## Changing the Meeting Time

### The Challenge

Whether working from the office or home, meetings are often changed. A frequent question we receive from EAs and PAs is 'What is the easiest way to change and update a meeting, especially if it is a recurring meeting?'

### The Solution

There are several ways to do this depending on whether or not a new date has been agreed upon.

### Microsoft Outlook 365 for Windows and Mac

*Updating/changing a meeting to an agreed new date and time*

Open the existing meeting and simply update the date and time and click on Send Update.

*Recurring meetings*

Changes to recurring meetings require a little more attention to detail.

For Microsoft Outlook (Windows):

1. Click on the date of the meeting which you need to change.

2. You are asked whether to change just this one or the series. Select 'Just this one'.

3. Click OK.

4. Make the necessary changes and click Send Update.

---

**Pro Tip:**

If you need to keep the meetings previous to this one intact as a record, yet change all subsequent meetings, end it at the last conforming meeting and create a new recurring meeting with the new frequency, start and end times.

---

For Microsoft Outlook (Mac):

1. Click on Meeting.

2. To change the details of either the whole series or just that date, use the Edit Series button.

3. To cancel the series, use the Cancel button, click on the down arrow and choose what you want to do.

## Google Workspace (G Suite)

1. From the Calendar app, click the event.

2. Click the pencil icon at the top to edit.

3. Change the meeting time and/or recurrence pattern.

4. Click Save.

5. Confirm 'This and following events' or 'All events.'

6. On the next dialogue, enter a note (optional) and update guests, or choose 'Don't Send.'

## Pro Tips

### *External guests*

If the meeting involves external people, you can send a portion of your executive's calendar by email instead of typing the dates separately.

1. Open a new email.

2. Click on Insert/Calendar.

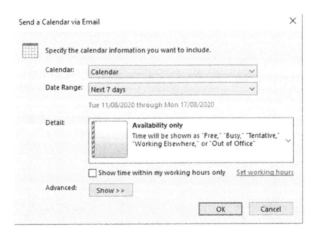

3.  Complete the range of dates within which you are looking and that portion of the calendar is automatically inserted in the email showing just 'busy' and 'tentative' as shown below.

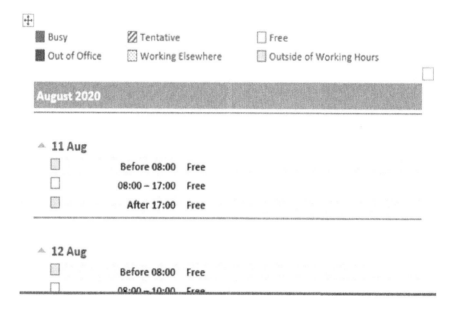

## *Finding a new date and time before changing the meeting*

In Outlook and Google Calendar, you have options for finding a new meeting time open on attendees' calendars. In Outlook, use either the Scheduling Assistant or the Room Finder. Both will show you best times to reschedule.

In Google Calendar, in edit mode on an event, click the Find a Time tab.

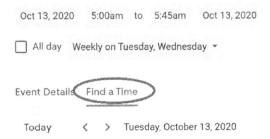

## *Another tip for determining new dates for meetings*

In the Windows version of Outlook, the calendar has some sentence recognition when it comes to forward planning. For example, it recognises words like 'five days' on and specific holidays like New Year, Independence Day and Halloween. This is very useful when you want to put in a follow-up meeting/reminder because in essence it helps you search rather than surf.

1.  Open the Go To Date box – Ctrl+G. In the top Date section, type 'After 14 August'.

2.  The cursor automatically takes you to that point in the calendar, in this case 14 August. Outlook recognises the following words, so you can use a combination such as 'Before 14 August', 'Next week' or 'Last week of October'.

3.  Warning do not leave unnecessary spaces when typing a phrase such as 'After 14 September' and spell the words correctly. Otherwise it may send the following error message: 'You must specify a valid date and time. Check your entries in the dialogue box...'

# | Tip #81 |

## Redirect Replies to Meeting Invitations

### The Challenge

You're the one setting up the meeting, but someone else is processing the RSVPs and making preparations. The person whom you support likes to set up her own meetings, but wants you to deal with the responses. You set up meetings from your executive's calendar but need to make sure he isn't dealing with the influx of accepts and declines.

These situations all have the same solution: redirecting.

### The Solution

Microsoft Outlook allows you to redirect replies to a meeting you set up to someone else. It's a little bit hidden, so if you never knew you could do it, don't feel badly. Here's what you do.

1.  From the meeting invitation in edit mode, click on File, then Properties.

# Strategy Meeting

**Move to Folder ⌄**

### Move item to a different folder

Move or copy this item to a different folder.

- Current Folder: Calendar

**Properties**

### Properties

Set and view advanced options and properties for this item.

- Size: Not yet saved

2. In the dialogue that appears, look for the Delivery Options section and check 'Have replies sent to.'

3. Click Select Names and choose to whom to redirect replies. That's it!

---

**Pro Tip:**

You can't do the same thing with an email message. From a composed email, click the Options tab and look in the More Options group for the Direct Replies To button.

---

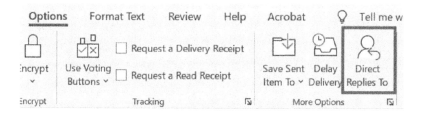

Mac users – this function is not available. You can work around it by setting up a rule to forward replies. Use the Subject Contains, Accept, Decline, Tentative. You may also need to add Yes, No, Maybe, etc. to accommodate responses which might come from another email client, e.g. Hotmail.

Although the responses will go to both the original sender and the nominated person (e.g. you as EA), it saves the other person having to forward email messages and maybe missing some.

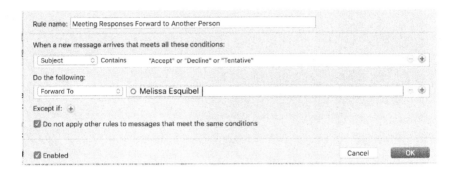

# Tip #82

## To Forward or Not to Forward a Meeting Invite

### The Challenge

How often have you set up a meeting only to find one of the invitees has forwarded the invite to someone not on your original list? Maybe you have done the same to a colleague? For the organiser, this can be annoying, they may have a reason for not inviting the other person. What is best practice for forwarding meeting invites? Is there a way to politely prevent people from forwarding invites?

### The Solution

Clearly, there may be many valid reasons for forwarding an invite - for example, you cannot attend and want someone to attend in your absence, there is someone else who is more knowledgeable and perhaps appropriate to attend instead of you or, maybe you feel a key person has been missed off the list.

To forward an invite without asking the meeting organiser is like passing on an invite to an exclusive event, like a birthday party or wedding. The organiser is then faced with the embarrassing situation of having to decline the new guest, perhaps because there is not space or food or to avoid a clash with someone with whom they do not get on.

## The Etiquette

Best practice is to always ask the meeting organiser before forwarding an invite. Tell them why you feel the other person should be invited.

Technology, too, can help you. In Outlook, you can prevent a meeting from being forwarded if the recipients are also using a current version of Outlook.

## Microsoft Outlook 365 for Windows and Mac

The default in Outlook is to allow meetings to be forwarded: you can prevent it as follows.

1. Set up the meeting invite in the usual way.
2. From the ribbon, open the Response Options drop-down menu and untick 'Allow forwarding'.

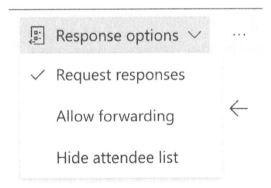

Be warned, if they are either using an old version of Outlook or other email application such as Gmail, the technology cannot help you. In this situation, you must specify in the invitation not to forward the invite without asking.

# Tip #83

## Additional Personal Calendars

## The Challenge

I once heard someone say, 'You are one person; you should have one calendar.' I don't know that I wholeheartedly disagree, but the ability to have additional personal calendars might be helpful for obligations you have outside of work which may affect how you schedule your work obligations. For example, would being able to see the following events alongside your work commitments help you schedule more effectively?

- Children's scheduled activities (sports, camp, lessons)
- Ongoing medical appointments
- Spouse's travel schedule
- Night classes
- Early morning fitness schedule

## The Solution

Using the ability to overlay your calendar in Outlook, you can overlay your work schedule on top of all of these and, for example, allow a little extra time to be perfectly presentable on the days you begin swimming laps in the pool and/or not schedule meetings that tend to go late on days your daughter has a track meet.

A couple of different approaches to consider:

1. Have one «Family Event» or «Personal Event» calendar that has all of these types of appointments. Use categories to differentiate between them.

2. Have a calendar for each type of event, such as Children's Activities, Classes or Lee's Travel Schedule.

The second approach allows you to be more selective about which personal or family events you are considering in a particular calendaring decision.

## Create Additional Calendars

1. Click on the Open Calendar button in the Manage Calendar group on the Home tab.
2. Select Create New Blank Calendar from the drop down menu.
3. Name it and be sure Calendar is selected in the dialogue box that appears.

## Arrange Your Overlay View

1. Check the boxes in the Navigation pane on the left to select the calendars you wish to see.
2. Initially, they will pop up next to each other in a sort of tiled view. If the view switches to Schedule View (may happen after selecting more than four calendars), simply click the Month, Week or Work Week view in the ribbon and continuing selecting calendars.
3. When you have the calendars you would like, click the block arrow to the left of the calendar name. You'll notice that they will start to appear layered one on top of the other.

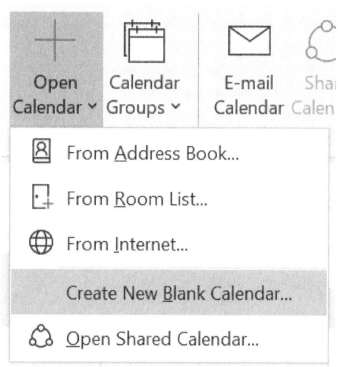

# | Tip #84 |

## Paper vs. Digital Diary

## The Challenge

An EA who has been using a paper-based diary for many years posed the question: 'Is it time for me to switch to an electronic one? I am technically very literate and use an electronic diary for managing my executive, but I adore my paper diary'.

Over the past decade, sales of paper journals (diaries) have grown from £23 million in 2011 to £38.8 million in 2016 and still growing (see www.statista.com). Inflation alone does not account for this level of growth. Indeed, a quick look on social media will show you plenty of feeds promoting paper-based journals. So, what is the solution to our EAs dilemma? Is there one?

## The Solution

There really is no right or wrong. Consider these pros and cons.

This is seen through the eyes of the author, who recently found her first Filofax diary from 1989. Yes, all the last 30+ years' copies are all neatly stored in a cabinet and serve as a memory bank rather like a photo album.

## Pros

- Easy to use and never runs out of juice and work regardless of the speed of the available Wi-Fi.

- Checking them late at night does not disturb sleep patterns as they don't emit any blue light.

- The process of writing helps the memory. Again, this has been supported by research.

- You can remain focused, with no chance of being disrupted when writing an entry by on screen social media or new email messages and alerts.

- Safe from cyber-criminals.

## Cons

- It could be lost or stolen.

- There is no easy back-up solution.

- It takes more time to enter recurring events by hand rather than setting up automatically.

- There are no automatic reminders. Reminders for things like renewing a phone contract or reconsidering an annual subscription are written in the diary.

- It may mean carrying an extra item (phone plus diary). Or, if you don't take your diary with you when you leave your home or office, it may mean that scheduling appointments has to wait until return.

- It is not as easily shared.

- You will need to purchase a new one every year, though it is typically no more than an up-market coffee.

- Making schedule changes might take more time. (TIP: If you choose a paper diary, write your entries in pencil so they can be rubbed out if the date changes.)

# LOOKING AFTER YOURSELF
# AND THE PLANET

# | Tip #85 |

## Top Tips to Protect Your Overall Wellbeing in the Digital Age

## The Challenge

Digital devices are addictive, and never more than when you are clearing the inbox, in a video conference or dealing with social media. Part of this book was written during the Covid-19 lock-down when video-conferencing and virtual events really took off. If you were not careful, you would find yourself spending 8+ hours a day wedded to your desk, jumping from video conference calls to checking email messages and social media.

That desk may not have been a conventional one but rather a kitchen table or comfortable chair with a device balanced on your knees (laptop, tablet, mobile phone). We are starting to see a rise in eye strain and musculo skeletal injuries such as back problems and strained wrists.

These are health issues that have long been related to excessive and poor use of computers. White working from home for extensive periods and in a time of great anxiety and uncertainty, it was all to easy too forget the basic principles of how to reduce the risk of eye strain and musculo skeletal injuries associated with excessive use of computer and digital devices (of all shapes and sizes).

Often these injuries are hidden and go unnoticed for a long while until you suffer a serious decline in your productivity, and even then it can take a while to trace the effects back to over-use of digital devices.

## The Solution

Here are seven top tips to reduce the havoc that digital devices can wreak on your physical and mental wellbeing.

1.  Move completely away from your desk at least twice a day, preferably for at least 20 to 30 minutes and, if possible, exercise to re-energise yourself, either when you start to feel tired or just as part of your natural break. Take a short walk, or if you are more sporty, try running. Alternatively, do some stretching or yoga to clear your mind.

2.  Try to avoid eating at your desk and over your keyboard/device. Keyboards don't respond well to food and drink spilt on them. Surveys also show that one in five keyboards harbour more germs than a toilet seat.

3.  Drink small amounts of water often during the day. Ideally you should drink about 1.5 litres of water per day. This not only helps to keep your body hydrated but also stops your throat (and hence voice) from drying up and becoming croaky.

4.  Avoid too much caffeine. While many find it a great energiser, remember it stays in your body for up to six hours. Consider avoiding it late in your working day. 400mg of caffeine per day is the recommended guideline, which is equivalent to four coffees/ teas, 10 cans of cola or two 'energy shot' drinks like Red Bull. Remember a chocolate drink counts as one of your four caffeinerelated drinks a day. The acceptable level of caffeine also depends on your weight – the lighter you are, the lower the dose should be. For a useful calculator, see: www.caffeineinformer.com/caffeine-safe-limits

5. Snack on healthy foods (for example, nuts, fruit and especially berries and health bars). Chocolate in moderation is also a good source of energy, but you may find yourself on a roller coaster -up for an hour after and then down again as the effects wear off. Avoid junk food.

6. Learn to power nap to recharge your batteries. To be effective, you need to decide if you are a Lark (early bird) or Owl (night worker) and time your nap accordingly. For Larks, between 1:00 and 1:30 p.m. is often the optimum. For Owls, closer to 2:30 to 5.30 p.m. might be better.

7. Switch off all technology devices at least one hour before going to sleep. Computer screens have been found to disturb sleep patterns, as they affect our melatonin levels which in turn affect our circadian rhythm. See 'Email Detox to Improve Performance and Wellbeing.'

# Tip #86

## Protect Your Muscles and Limbs in the Digital Age

## The Challenge

Ever experienced back pain, sore fingers or a sharp pain in your wrist? These are all symptoms of repetitive strain injuries associated with excessive use of a keyboard. They take their toll on your wellbeing regardless of the type of device. Indeed, in the early days of mobile phones (and for those who remember the Blackberry). sore thumb syndrome was a well-known problem. One of us speaks from the heart after suffering De Quervain's tenosynovitis (inflammation of the joints between the thumb and wrist). The treatment involved injections and wearing a wrist splint for several months. Everything from typing a short email to drying one's hair took time and was painful; worse still, no golf.

Then there is telephone neck strain (TNS) from resting the phone under your neck (regardless of device type).

## The Solution

Here are 15 tips to help you preserve and protect your limbs and muscles and hence maintain your productivity.

## How You Sit

1. Sit up straight and check that your back is properly supported. Use your chair's back rest to help you. Avoid slumping over the keyboard.

2. Sit at the right height. Your arms should form an L shape with the forearms resting horizontally in front of the keyboard. Avoid sitting either too low or too high, as this too encourages you to tilt forward and slouch.

3. Keep your feet flat on the floor. Use a foot-rest if needed, especially if you are short and your feet don't touch the floor. Avoid either tucking them under your chair or lowering the chair, as this can cause muscle tension on the arms. Being properly positioned helps your back and stops muscle tension in the ankles.

4. Think right angles (90º) for your knees, elbows and hips. These should be open at just over 90º.

5. Set the monitor at the right height – eye level. The top of the screen (monitor) should be just level with your eyes (for a 15 to 17 inch one). Too low and you will be slouching as you move away from the chair to see the screen and putting undue strain on your neck muscles.

6. For touch typists, try raising the monitor so that the top section is just visible below eye level. For those who 'hunt and peck' and need to see the keyboard, try having the monitor a fraction lower to reduce unnecessary raising and lowering of the head.

7. Check that the screen is at the optimum distance – an arm's length away from you.

8. Keep the keyboard and mouse close at hand. Ideally, your keyboard should be four to six inches from the front of the desk (to allow your wrists to be properly supported). Stretching each time for the mouse will put undue strain on your shoulder muscles and spine.

9. For laptop users, having a separate mouse is better if you are using the laptop for prolonged periods.

## Using the Keyboard

10. Type using a neutral wrist position. Check that your hands are properly supported and rest properly on the keyboard. Try to avoid bending your thumbs and little finger and arching your wrist upwards. Wrist rests can be useful, but make sure you don't rest your wrists unnecessarily on them when typing, otherwise you may find your wrists are arched and too high. The rest should only be used when not typing.

11. Keep the keyboard as flat as possible. It should be either flat or below your elbow. Just because a keyboard can be adjusted upwards, does not mean that this is better.

12. Go lightly – hit the keys lightly. Most users hit the keyboard four times harder than necessary, thus putting undue strain on the wrists and fingers.

13. Avoid pressing hard on your wrist and especially on the pulse area, as this can restrict the flow of blood to the hand and increase the risk of injury.

## Other Considerations

14. De-clutter your desk and make it easy to access anything else you frequently use, (for example, your phone). Repeated stretching to reach the phone, papers, and other items will put strain on your back and shoulder.

15. Use a headset/headphones rather than a handset if you often use the phone while working at a computer. This significantly reduces the chance of straining your neck muscles and getting telephone neck syndrome (TNS). If you prefer the handset, then use your non-writing hand to minimise the risk of TNS.

Adopting some of these as appropriate to your role and environment will help you maintain if not boost your productivity as you keep your vital muscles and limbs in tip-top shape.

# | Tip #87 |

## Protect Your Eyes in the Digital Age

Other tips have dealt with protecting your overall wellbeing in the digital age and reducing the scope for damage to your bones and muscles. This tip focuses specifically on how to protect your eyes.

## The Challenge

Spending too long looking at a digital device can do serious harm to your eyesight. The classic symptoms of computer vision syndrome (CVS), as it is known, are dry eyes, itchy eyes and headaches.

Too much exposure to blue light can increase your age-related risk of macular degeneration which can ultimately lead to blindness. The current evidence suggests that it is not direct exposure to the blue light but rather its impact on other aspects of your wellbeing, such as stress and lack of sleep.

## The Solution

Whether the risks to your visual capacity are short or long term, here are nine very simple yet important steps you can take to mitigate these risks.

1. Adopt the 20:20:20 rule. Look away from the screen and focus on a point 20 feet (6 meters) away for at least 20 seconds every 20 minutes. Repeat this exercise at least three times when you take a break.

2. Blink often. This helps keep your eyes moist.

3. Don't keep the screen too close to your face. The idea is to have the screen at arm's length.

4. Have the screen at either eye level or just below.

5. Tilt the screen to reduce glare and reflections.

6. Use the brightness control to adjust the screen's brightness to suit your needs and comfort. A special blue light filter such as Ocushield can be of help, making looking at the actual screen easier on the eyes.

7. Change font sizes until you are comfortable, be that for viewing webpages, documents, presentations, etc. Remember, squinting at the screen puts an unnecessary added strain on your eye muscles.

8. Place the screen such that your main light source (e.g. the window) is not shining into your eyes as you look at the screen. If you do have a window behind the screen, use a blind to reduce the level of direct light shining into your eyes, especially UV from sunlight.

9. If you are reading a long article or document, consider reading offline and on paper. Despite sounding un-green, not surprisingly many of us still find reading printed media easier than on-screen text.

Although the damage from too much exposure to digital devices is rarely permanent, the symptoms can lead to excessive tiredness and moodiness, which in turn reduce your productivity and ability to perform. These nine tips will help you stay in top form.

# Tip #88

## Managing Distractions – The Causes

> *"A wealth of information means a dearth of*
> *something else… a poverty of attention."*
> *- H. Simon, 1971*

## The Challenge

'I find it very hard to start a substantial task (for example, writing up the board minutes, preparing a presentation for my executive). Once started, it is easy to be distracted by new email, social media alerts, grabbing a coffee. By the end of the day, I've probably completed half the task. To complete it, I either need to stay late or start early the next day. Sometimes, and even more stressfully, what was a high priority task now becomes urgent, too. How can I stop being distracted and stay focused?'

## The Solution

### The Cost of Distractions

This is a common problem for most of us. Distractions are expensive both in terms of our personal productivity and our wellbeing.

For example, it is estimated that being distracted by each new email alert adds about 15 minutes to the time needed to complete the task on which you were originally focused. This is due to the time it takes the brain to readjust to the original task.

Many studies have shown that distractions reduce our productivity, wellbeing and work-life balance. Other studies have found that distractions distort how our brain functions: some even think it reduces our critical thinking powers. And we have yet to see the true long-term effect on our brains. Indeed, one study found that continuous checking of email and text messages caused people's IQ to drop by 10 points.

Whatever the outcome, we do know that interruptions and distractions invariably mean we don't finish the tasks we must do during the day and consequently we have to work outside normal hours, which puts a strain on our wellbeing and relationships.

In 2005, it was estimated that being interrupted by new email alerts alone cost the US economy $588 billion per year (see The Cost of Not Paying Attention: How Interruptions Impact Knowledge Workers Productivity' by Spira and Feintuch). That was pre-social media alerts and Covid-19. We can assume that now, in 2021, the overall financial cost is much higher.

Fortunately, there are a number of actions you can take to help you stay focused and apps which can support you.

## Why Do You Allow Yourself to Be Distracted?

The first step is to identify why you allow yourself to be distracted. For example:

- The task is perceived as difficult - answering email messages and checking social media posts is easier.
- Fear of missing out (FOMO) – you feel you must check email and social media posts.
- Addiction – you must have your 'fix' of email and social media.
- Self gratification.

- You're not in the mood – perhaps the task requires a level of creativity of which you're not, at the moment, feeling capable. During Covid-19, many people reported finding it hard to concentrate because of the uncertainty.
- You feel you must fill every moment of the day, so as you go from meeting to meeting (physical or virtual), you feel you must do something to fill the void time and therefore check your email notifications and social media posts.

## Self-Assessment Exercise

First, each time you feel the urge to be distracted, write down how you feel and what you feel is driving that urge. Second, put a price, quantitative or qualitative, on the cost of the distraction - for example, missing seeing a loved one, not going to the gym, the effect on the quality of your sleep from working late into the night.

Only when you have identified what triggers the distractions and their cost can you really start to reduce them and stay focused.

# Tip #89

## Managing Distractions – Staying Focused for Longer

### The Challenge

Now that we know why we get distracted ('Managing Distractions – The Causes'), the challenge is to stay focused for longer.

### The Solution

There is a multitude of tips and advice on how to stay focused Some solutions depend on the reasons why we allow ourselves to be distracted. Here are our top 10 universal solutions, whatever the reason.

1. Plan your day – What are your goals? What tasks must you complete (and be realistic)? Do the planning at either the start of the day or end of the previous one. For many, doing it at the start of the day is marginally better because it allows for the unexpected to be requested by your executives.

2. Use either the Pomodoro or Time Box principle to handle the day's workload. Pomodoro means staying focused on the task at hand for about 20 minutes. Then take a short break or switch tasks briefly (for example, check the inbox). Time Box

is about allocating specific portions of the day during which you focus just on a specific task.

3.  Turn off all the new email, social media and collaborative platform alerts, such as notifications from Teams, notice boards and Twitter

4.  For social media and collaborative platforms, if you want to see the alerts, set up a rule to automatically send these to a folder outside the main inbox.

5.  Make time to check your email, social media posts and collaborative platform alerts.

6.  When starting a new task, break it down into small bite-sized chunks.

7.  Reward yourself as you complete each small part (even if it is only with a drink of coffee or piece of chocolate).

8.  Manage your calendar to create free time to do the task.

9.  Create a distraction-free work environment (at home or in a formal office). That might mean clearing your desk of all items likely to distract you, including your mobile phone.

10. Wait 10 minutes after you feel the urge to be distracted. Often the urge to turn away from the task at hand then passes, leaving you focused. If need be, write down the nagging thought as a way to dismiss it from your memory and help your brain stay focused.

## Apps to Help You Stay Focused

There is now an array of apps to help you stay focused with new ones being added all the time. Currently these are our seven favourites:

1.  **Forest** – Each time you are distracted and check your phone, you are charged, and the money goes towards planting a tree.

2.  **LeechBlock** lets you block access to a specific web site, such as Facebook.

3.  **Mindful Browsing** nudges you away from surfing unnecessary web-sites.

4. **RescueTime** – This one both tracks the time you spend on different apps and blocks access to websites.
5. **Timely** tracks how you spend your time.
6. **Pocket** is a bookmaking tool which saves web pages for you to read offline later.
7. **Flora** – Based on the Pomodoro principle, it plants a virtual seed on your screen which grows the longer you stay focused.

## Increased Productivity from Staying Focused

There are surprisingly few studies which quantify the gains. However, we do know that time is saved: this could be the difference between being seen as super-efficient instead of inefficient. Clients often report that simply by switching off the new email alert they are able to stop working on time if not earlier.

To turn off email notifications in Outlook:
1. On the File tab, click Options.
2. Select the Mail category.
3. Scroll down to Message Arrival and uncheck 'Display a desktop alert'.

There is also improved wellbeing, less stress (and hence time off sick) and better work-life balance which is hard to quantify. Ultimately, this might be saving a relationship which might otherwise result in divorce.

General

**Mail**

Calendar

People

Tasks

Search

**Message arrival**

When new messages arrive:

☐ Play a sound

☐ Briefly change the mouse pointer

☑ Show an envelope icon in the taskbar

☐ Display a Desktop Alert

# ‖ Tip #90 ‖

## Email Detox to Improve Performance and Wellbeing

*You cannot change the habits of a lifetime and the rewards you gain from them but you can change the process by which you receive the reward.*
*— Charles Duhigg*

## The Challenge

An EA to a vice president in a global organisation recently commented that she felt she never really disconnected from her inbox even when on leave. She felt she was constantly checking her email messages and asked how she could disconnect both late at night and on vacation.

## The Solution

This is a question we are frequently asked, especially in the 24x7x365 working environment and even more so during the Covid-19 pandemic. The starting point is to ask yourself why you keep checking your inbox: then we can look at top tips to disconnect.

## Why Do You Keep Checking Your Inbox?

There are four principal reasons why people are constantly checking their inbox and email messages.

1. Email Addiction – Like any form of addiction from alcohol to shopping, there is a sense of reward which gives you a buzz after the action, in this case checking email messages.

2. Fear of missing out (FOMO) – What might you be missing out on? This is especially true for social messages? Underlying this is generally a sense of insecurity. This is exacerbated in times of turmoil such as the Covid-19 pandemic.

3. Perceived expectation that you are always available – It is always interesting to ask who expects you to be constantly checking your inbox. The response is often either that it's the organisational culture or the executive expects an instant response. However, when we ask the executive, they frequently say they do not have such an expectation. That said, there are some executives who say that this is the nature of the business.

4. Overwhelmed with email messages - The feeling that the only way to keep up is to keep checking.

There is a growing body of research which shows there are two main impacts of constantly checking your email messages on performance.

1. Distractions – We have discussed this previously in our two chapters on Managing Distraction. It takes between one and twenty minutes to refocus after being distracted by a new email message.

2. Blue light suppresses melatonin which is the hormonal key to a good night's sleep. Your brain does not have a proper rest. Answering email messages and checking social media makes the brain feel like it needs to keep working. It is therefore imperative if you want to retain peak performance that you

have an inbox detox every day - that is, periods when you disconnect from all your digital devices.

## An Inbox Detox – Ten Top Tips

The underlying golden principles are, first, you cannot change your habits, as Charles Duhigg of 'The Power of Habit' tells us: you must stick to the old habits and old rewards, but you can change the routine that delivers those rewards. Second, your behaviour and attitudes will influence those with whom you work.

Based on these golden rules, here are 10 ways you can create an inbox detox for a block of time each day.

## Addiction

Identify why you keep checking your inbox. Use a self-assessment tool to benchmark your level of addiction at https://www.mesmo.co.uk/assess-yourself/email-addiction-self-audit/. If you are addicted, these are the steps you should take to reduce your level of addiction.

a) Set a realistic goal for reducing the number of times you check your messages each day.
b) As soon as you have the urge to check the inbox, pause and do something else which will eventually give you the same level of satisfaction (or buzz). For example, sip a drink of water, hum a tune, start to draw.
c) Lengthen the time between checking the inbox. For example, add on a couple minutes each day until you find you can delay checking for about 45 minutes.
d) Reward yourself each time you reach the daily goal you set yourself. Conversely, fine yourself when you fail.

If you are addicted, the change may take time and you might need someone to help you. Sadly, at the time of writing there is no inbox addiction support group like we have for alcohol and substance abuse.

However, we are thinking of setting up one, as inbox addiction is just as damaging to your health and social wellbeing. Stay tuned!

## Organisational Culture and Other People's Expectations

For those for whom the underlying cause is not addiction, here are nine actions you can take.

1.  Set boundaries outside of which you do not deal with work email messages.

2.  Agree with your colleagues and executive on how they can contact you if something is really urgent and cannot wait. See Communicating 'Urgent'.

3.  Use your Out of Office message if need be to manage senders' expectations.

4.  Switch off at least one hour before going to bed.

5.  Leave all digital devices outside the bedroom.

6.  Keep pen and paper by the bed if you need to make notes (for example, your mind is churning with things to do tomorrow).

7.  Use a conventional alarm clock rather than the one in your digital device.

8.  Read a conventional paper-based book rather than e-book.

9.  Provide support and training for colleagues.

In this way you can help establish a better organisational email culture. The more people with whom you can engage in altering both your own behaviour and the organisational culture, the faster the change will happen. Indeed, some organisations and countries have now recongised the positive effect which disconnecting from your inbox has on performance and have taken significant action. For example, in France and Germany they are making it illegal for managers to expect lower level workers to answer email messages outside of normal working hours. Some companies (such as Daimler Benz) have developed software which returns messages when people are on leave and ask the sender to re-send the message on their return.

Don't just sit there feeling you must always be connected to your inbox. Speak out and lead in the quest for a daily digital detox.

## Email Message Overload

If you are simply suffering from email message overload, then start to audit your inbox to reduce the volume of messages (see 'Audit Your Inbox to Find the Root Cause of Cc'd Email Messages'), use rules to filter out unnecessary ones (see 'Outlook Rules Rule!' or 'Rules Rule: Gmail Filters') and look at managing your time at the inbox more efficiently. If you still need an email message detox, then obviously you need to follow the top tips above.

# ❙ Tip #91 ❙

## Brain Food to Maintain Productivity

*One cannot think well, love well, sleep well, if one has not dined well.*
*— Virginia Woolf*

## The Challenge

With a busy work and social life, finding time to eat a traditional three-course lunch or dinner can be hard. Snacking is often the option for many - snacking between meetings, feeding children, shopping, catching up with work after the children are asleep and so on. A good diet is one of the keys to your overall ability to perform at your best.

The bookshops (real and virtual) are brimming with cookery books. Many newsletters devote at least a section each week to dietary matters. Forgive the pun, but picking the wheat from the chaff can take time, and the foods and snacks you most love may not be the best for your health. What are the most nourishing foods which ideally should always be to hand?

# The Solution

There are two main areas of food on which this tip focuses: those to help improve your memory and brain power and those to give you energy.

In the case of brain food, it is often also about reducing the risk of memory loss. In the case of energy, foods that keep hunger at bay such as those rich in fibre and protein, as well as those that boost your energy, are valuable in this quest.

## Different Carbohydrates

Carbohydrates are essential to our wellbeing but not all are equal. There are two types, good and bad. The bad ones are high in refined sugar. They give you an energy surge which quickly fades away and often leaves you feeling down, at a level below that at which you were before you ate the item. Examples of these are candy, sugary drinks, cakes and biscuits (cookies). The bad carbohydrates are often the food we crave for when we are feeling hungry, depressed, angry or otherwise emotional in a negative sense. Good sugars release their carbohydrate content slowly, which means your energy levels stay up longer and drop much more slowly.

## Vitamins

According to Harvard Medical School, B6, B9 and B12 can help break down homocysteine, high levels of which have been associated with a greater risk of dementia and Alzheimer's disease. B vitamins also help produce energy needed to develop new brain cells. Vitamin C helps the immune system, and vitamin K has been linked to regulating calcium in the brain. (See https://www.ncbi.nlm.nih.gov/pmc/articles/PMC6436180/)

## Fatty Acids and Antioxidants

In recent studies, such as 'Fatty Acids, Antioxidants and Physical Activity in Brain Aging' (https://www.ncbi.nlm.nih.gov/pmc/articles/ PMC5707735/), certain fatty acids (omega-3 and omega-6) and antioxidants have been shown to positively affect brain health and control brain aging. While this area of nutrition and brain health is still being studied, these indications can inform your food choices.

## Always Check With Your Doctor!

Before trying anything new, you must check carefully that it doesn't interfere with any existing medication or conditions. For example, cranberries are deemed to be great for boosting your immune system but are to be avoided for anyone on either blood thinning medication or vitamin K supplements because they increase the effect of the former and decrease that of the latter.

All food and no water and you will not benefit from what you eat. Stay hydrated – see Tips 7.1 and 7.2.

---

**Pro Tip:**

It has been said that one should 'eat breakfast like a king, lunch like a princess and dinner like a pauper'. Most health experts still swear by this principle, which was invented by Adelle Davis, an American who is regarded as one of the greatest modern-day nutritionists.

---

## Top 21 Foods for Boosting Health and Productivity

The 21 foods listed here are the ones which nearly all food and health experts are agreed on. That doesn't mean that if you have a favourite which works for you that's not on the list, then it's wrong. Far from it. We could write a book on this subject. What we have tried to do here is give you an overview.

| | Food | Beneficial Characteristics |
|---|---|---|
| 1 | Nuts (especially walnuts) | Omega-3 fatty acids, protein and vitamin |
| 2 | Blueberries | Antioxidants |
| 3 | Blackcurrants | Vitamin C and other compounds linked to reducing inflammation |
| 4 | Strawberries | Vitamin C, antioxidants and minerals |
| 5 | Avocados | Fibre, variety of vitamins and good fats |
| 6 | Apples | Fibre, variety of vitamins which are released slowly |
| 7 | Oranges | Vitamin C |
| 8 | Broccoli | Vitamin K |
| 9 | Sweet potatoes (including yams) | Good carbohydrates and fibre |
| 10 | Dark leafy greens (Spinach, kale, some types of cabbage) | Protein, vitamins especially vitamin K and minerals |
| 11 | Beetroot | Folic acid, minerals, tryptophan important to the manufacture of serotonin |
| 12 | Tomatoes | Minerals, vitamins, antioxidants, especially lycopene |
| 13 | Sage | Antioxidant-rich |
| 14 | Pumpkin seeds | Vitamin B, minerals such as magnesium, zinc |
| 15 | Whole grains (Whole cereals which contain all their component parts, such as bran, and have not been refined) | Vitamin E, B vitamins |
| 16 | Lentils | Fibre and protein |
| 17 | Fatty fish (Salmon, tuna, trout and sardines) | Omega-3 fatty acids |
| 18 | Coffee | Caffeine, antioxidants (Warning: Too much can leave you jittery and unable to concentrate) |
| 19 | Dark chocolate | Good carbohydrates and antioxidants |
| 20 | Camomile/ chamomile tea | Apigenin (antioxidant) |
| 21 | Eggs | B vitamins, protein, zinc, iron |

# ‖ Tip #92 ‖

## Keep Screen Time in Check

*Your morning sets up the success of your day. So many people wake up and immediately check text messages, email messages and social media. I use my first hour awake for my morning routine of breakfast and meditation to prepare myself.*
*- Caroline Ghosn*

## The Challenge

Do you ever feel you have spent all day looking at a computer (or mobile) screen but are not quite sure if you have spent that time wisely? Most of us feel that way at some point or another during the week. Even if you are working on a specific screen-based project, the chances are that you may have had at least four or five applications open, checked your email messages at least 10 times during the day and probably did not stay focused for more than 10 minutes.

Recent surveys from Microsoft now suggest that older workers find it easier to stay focused than millennials and Generation Z ('The Future of Work – The Good, the Challenging and the Unknown.' by J. Spataro, VP for Microsoft 365, July 2020.). None of this makes you productive. Indeed, the opposite is a more likely outcome, as one's wellbeing is affected negatively. For example, spending too much time in front of a screen can:

- Re-engineer your brain, making it harder to think strategically
- Increase the likelihood of depression
- Reduce one's ability to connect (socialize) effectively with people
- Lower the ability to process information as information overload sets it

The key is to decide what is a productive use of our time at the screen.

## The Solution

The starting point is to quantify (audit) how you really spend your time when looking at a computer (or even mobile device) screen. Reality is often very different from one's perception.

## What to Measure

You need to know not just exactly how much time you really spend in front of a screen all day, but also, for instance:

- How long do you stay focused before switching applications - for example, from preparing a document to processing email?
- Who are the colleagues with whom you are in most contact (be it by email, text, app)?
- Are the people with whom you are in most frequent contact the right ones for you and your role?
- How many applications are open at any one time?
- Which applications do you use the most often and for how long?
- For what portion of the working day do you switch off from the screen and allow yourself quiet time?
- How early and late are you still online checking email, social media posts and other screen activities?

- How often do you check for new email, alerts and notifications?
- What is the balance of work and social screen time?

## Apps to Measure Screen Time

There is a range of apps to measure screen time, all of which measure different aspects of how you spend your time online. Some of our favourites are shown below.

| Desktop Apps | Mobile Apps |
| --- | --- |
| Microsoft MyAnalytics | Screen time - iOS |
| Screen Time – iOS Catalina | Dinner Mode – iOS |
| Freedom | Freedom |
| Zen Screen | Zen Screen |
| | Break Free |
| | Social Fever – Android |

Each has slightly different functionality. For example, Freedom includes a meditation app. Dinner Mode includes a timer which can be set to create screen-free time, for instance during mealtime. You can also use Dinner Mode to challenge yourself. You are awarded points for not breaking the screenfree barrier. You can also share your Dinner Mode results, set a game/competition with others and create a support group for those suffering with screen addiction. Zen Screen forces you off the device and shuts its down. Hence, it is important to clarify what you want to measure in detail rather than just how much time you spend online. Most apps carry a small cost. However, they all have a free version which gives you access to limited functions.

As in previous tips where we list apps, what is the best now as we write may be overtaken by a newcomer or upgrade to a competitor. This list simply serves to point you in the right direction. Two which stand out and are free are Microsoft MyAnalytics and Apple Screen Time. Both provide a wealth of data to help you identify how you spend your time and where you might need to refocus, albeit it in very different ways.

## Microsoft MyAnalytics

MyAnalytics is free for those with an Office 365 account. Not surprisingly, it is geared towards encouraging you to use more Microsoft products such as Teams: nonetheless, you can take away plenty of data to help you access how effectively you are using your time at the screen and especially in terms of the proportion of your time you spend with different people in your network.

1. Basic Weekly Report

Below is an example from Monica's MyAnalytics weekly report.

For that week, there were few meetings and email messages because she was focused on completing her half of the draft for this book and a project which did not involve meetings and chats, and a couple of rounds of golf.

2.  Discover More

Click on 'Discover more' and from the MyAnalytics website, use the left-hand menu to explore in more detail. For example, Network shows you the percentage of email messages sent to different people. Thus, you can identify if you are spending too much time emailing colleagues but not enough with clients, or maybe not sufficient time with key people who can help you develop your career.

Click on Wellbeing and you can see just how much quiet time you enjoyed. This was very revealing for Monica. Despite trying to switch off after 9:30 p.m., working from home often means using her Mac to do other things such as online banking and shopping. However, there was clearly quiet time away from the screen when on the golf course and visiting friends.

---

**Pro Tip:**

You can change days you work and the start and end time for your normal working day. Click on Config Settings – bottom left of the menu.

---

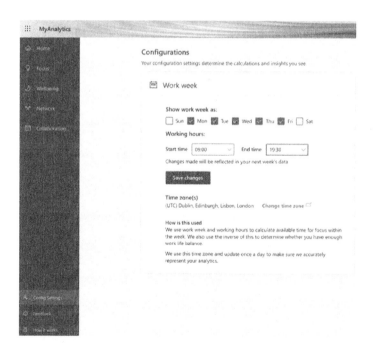

## Apple Screen Time

The apple Screen Time app is much more focused on the time spent online, the apps you use, the number of notifications and how quickly you pick them up. A typical summary report is shown below.

Again, it has a wealth of functions, including 'App Limits' and 'Downtime', which allow you to set boundaries for switching off. You can link all your iOS devices provided they are all on iCloud.

On balance, Screen Time is probably more useful if you are trying to break your addiction rather than see with whom you are spending time. For the latter, MyAnalytics is more useful.

## Interpreting the Results

Tools such as MyAnalytics clearly give you a very good overall picture, although as shown, there are flaws, in that time away from the office is not recorded as quiet time. It can be hard, too, to differentiate between time spent using an app like WhatsApp for business or social.

Nonetheless, it does quantify where you really spend your time rather than where you think you spend it. As such, it can help you identify where you might need to refocus your time, especially working from home when it might be more difficult than usual to develop your network and switch off.

## *Ten top tips for reducing and refocusing your screen time*

Establishing routine and goals is the key. Most successful people from artists to business-people have a routine and try to maintain it for the majority of time. Some might say this is verging on obsession. Here are our top 10 tips to help you focus your screen time and use it effectively regardless of the device used.

1. Use a screen time app to help you identify how you currently spend your time online.

2. Set SMART goals for what you want to achieve from your time online and indeed the day. If urgent tasks land on your desk, simply adjust your schedule for the day but don't abandon it, otherwise you will lose focus.

3. Create a routine at least for the start and finish of each day.

4. Set boundaries outside which you do not access your devices. Use your screen time management app to help you. These can be one or multiple boundaries (for example, start and end of the day, mealtimes, and out with friends). This quiet time gives you time to think and enjoy the moment.

5. Leave all devices outside the bedroom and bathroom.

6. Reduce the number of pop-up notifications you receive from new posts on social media. Alternatively, send them to a folder. (See 'Outlook Rules Rule!' and 'Rules Rule: Gmail Filters'.)

7. Limit the number of apps and news feeds to which you subscribe.
   This will help with Tip 6 above.

8. For iOS users – go Grey. It makes it harder to read the device and discourages you from spending too long looking at the screen.

9. Take your work email off your personal mobile device.

10. Join the Slow Movement (https://www.slowmovement.com/). Allow yourself to take time before checking for new notifications.

Ultimately, it is all about the quality, not the quantity, of time spent in front of the screen regardless of device type. This tip focuses on business, but it is important not to forget that time spent online for social and leisure reasons counts towards your daily dose of screen time. For example, whilst e-books are great, remember this too counts as screen time! Switching to paper books occasionally can help reduce the amount of leisure time you spend on a screen. Surprise a friend or family member with a phone call rather than a text.

# Tip #93

## Reduce Carbon Emissions from Digital Devices

*The carbon footprint of our gadgets, the internet and the systems supporting them accounts for about 3.7% greenhouse emissions globally. It is similar to the amount produced by the airline industry globally. These emissions are predicted to double by 2025.*
*- Mike Hazas, Lancaster University, in BBC's*
*'Smart Guide to Climate Change'*

## The Challenge

Dealing with climate change is a central concern not just for organisations and governments but for individuals too. It will be here as a challenge long after the Covid-19 pandemic comes to pass, albeit it will have changed the way we work. The question for you as readers of this book is, given our dependence on technology, how can we as individuals in the digital world help to reduce the level of carbon emissions?

## The Solution

Many of us have been taught that if we take care of the pennies, the pounds/dollars/euros will take care of themselves. This can be applied to contributing to the global reduction in carbon emissions. Here are 20 key ways you can help by working more effectively with digital technology without sacrificing your productivity. Indeed, in some cases it will help you improve it and might even make you stand out positively from the crowd.

1. Reduce the number and size of email messages you send each day. Processing email is probably one of the major source of carbon emissions. (See 'Email Management to Reduce Carbon Emissions'.)

2. Check how many email accounts you have and see if you can reduce them.

3. Keep your text messages simple and reduce the number and size of images sent. The bigger the image, the more $CO_2$ needed to process and send it.

4. Use a laptop rather than desktop, as laptops are about 80% more energy efficient.

5. Set your devices, desktop and mobile, to switch automatically to low energy/sleep mode when not in use.

6. At night, switch laptops and desktops to 'Sleep'/'Hibernate' rather than power it off. This will also protect the life of your device.

7. Switch off other digital devices when not in use and especially mobile phones if possible. This is also great for improving your wellbeing. (See 'Top Tips to Protect Your Overall Wellbeing in the Digital Age'.)

8. Reduce the amount you print, and if you do print, make sure it's double-sided. (One of us still had her printer in the original packaging a month after it was delivered!)

9. Turn down the level of screen brightness to an acceptable one. First, lower levels of brightness consume less power, and

second, it is better for your eyes (more restful and reduces eye strain).

10. Focus your searches. It is so easy to type in a few words in the search bar. If it doesn't reveal the right result, you just search again. But each search consumes energy. In 2015, Google estimated its data centres consumed about 5.7 terawatts of power, almost the same as the whole of San Francisco. One way to help reduce this is by thinking through your search terms more carefully before typing into the search bar. Don't be afraid to type whole questions or sentences in your search words. You will be more likely to get the results you want in the first try.

11. Install an ad blocker. In addition to improving cybersecurity, these also help in the fight against climate change. How? Adverts take up space and can slow download times, which in turn means you use more power to process a page.

12. Limit the amount of data tracking which websites demand. Several of the major search engines are now developing apps to help reduce the energy used and hence carbon emissions. For example, at the time of writing there is:

- Google's Chrome 'Earth Mode', which tracks your internet carbon footprint and Google then plant trees to neutralise it.

- Ecosia which donates web-based advertising revenue to organisations devoted to reducing carbon emissions.

- Firefox's Enhanced Tracking Protection is designed to reduce the level of tracking, although they do admit that if the boundaries are too tight the website might not function!

- DuckDuckGo doesn't track your activity the way the more popular search engines do. Not only do you get better privacy protection, but you don't use as much energy to process your searches.

13. Reduce your screen time. Simply use your devices less! (See 'Keep Screen Time in Check'.)

14. Limit your dependency on the cloud. Did we really say this? The key is to think through what you really need to store in the cloud. Again, with today's digital devices, it is so easy to simply let all your photos and files be automatically uploaded. But do you really need six different photos of the same item just from different angles? Or could you save just the best one in the cloud? The same goes for different versions of files and especially those with high resolution images.

15. Recycle devices when possible and safe to do so. Many large retailers, like Best Buy in the US, have recycling programs in their stores. Some states and municipalities also run electronics recycling events. Be sure to clean all data off your devices before recycling. The US Federal Trade Commission offers tips on what to do with your mobile devices before discarding or selling them (https://www.consumer.ftc.gov/articles/how-protect-your-phone-and-data-it).

16. Consider using a green mobile operator. The supplier will aim to use renewable energy and may also donate to a climate change organisation every time you make a call. At present these are few and far between there are a few in Germany and Austria. Nonetheless, it's an area to watch.

17. Switch to an environmentally friendly email service provider. They operate on a similar basis to mobile phone providers and, as per Tip 16, there are currently limited options but these will surely be more available over time.

18. Download rather than stream videos. Streaming means consuming energy each time you view the item whereas once downloaded it doesn't require the same level of carbon. Current estimates suggest streaming consumes 300 million tons of $CO_2$!Perhaps it's time to be more selective about what and how much you watch.

19. Block or disable video auto play and stop wasting time and energy watching videos that you didn't choose to watch. Depending on the browser, app and device you use, this can be done either in your settings or via an extension.

24. Don't feel you must always have the latest model of a device from smart phone to tablet. More often than not, more functions and faster speed means a higher carbon footprint as the device needs more processing power.

Individually we may only be talking about saving a few grams of $CO2$. Collectively, however, this will make a substantial and sustainable long-term contribution to reducing our digital $CO2$ emissions and help to arrest climate change.

# Tip #94

## Email Management to Reduce Carbon Emissions

*If every (business) email user in the (UK) were to send one less unnecessary email per day, that would reduce carbon emissions by 16,433 tonnes – equivalent to a staggering 81,152 flights from London Heathrow to Madrid.*
*– From 'How Bad Are Bananas? The Carbon Footprint of Everything' by Mike Burners-Lee*

## The Challenge

In 'Reduce Carbon Emissions from Digital Devices', we looked at the impact overall of our current and rising use of digital devices. Many have called for the end of email. Yet it holds the honour of being the most pervasive technology. Launched over 30 years ago by Mike Tomlinson, email is still alive. Volumes are predicted to grow at about 4% worldwide despite the arrival of many new types of digital communications. Perhaps not surprisingly, processing email is one of the most significant consumers of $CO_2$. To process and store one email costs about 4grams of $CO_2$. Add a medium to large attachment and it takes about 50grams of $CO_2$, a tenfold plus rise. Again, these are small footprints but just think about the carbon footprint of someone who receives about 100 email messages a week. Time and again during workshops and webinars, people tell us they only need about 60% of the email messages they receive.

What can we do as individuals to contribute to managing climate change through our use of email?

## The Solution

The big picture is minimalisation and remembering that deleting is not an option. You still burn $CO_2$. Here are 10 ways we can all manage our use of email more effectively to help reduce carbon emissions.

1.  Reduce the number of email messages you send each day. Before hitting Send, ask yourself: why am I sending this email? What will it achieve? If you don't have a good answer, don't send the email. If you do still need to send the email, then ask yourself if there is a better way to communicate this message - for example, by using a collaborative tool like Teams, especially if you are sending one message to many people. (See Tip 65, 'Consider Collaborative Tools', page 226.)

2.  Audit your (and your manager's) inbox to identify how you can reduce the number of email messages you receive, such as cc'd email messages, newsletters, etc. (see 'Audit Your Inbox to Find the Root Cause of Cc'd Email Messages'.)

3.  Share files rather than emailing them to individuals.

4.  Stop sending thank you email. Add a note of gratitude in the original email - for example, 'thanks in advance for your help'. If the person has gone the extra mile, call them to say thank you. It may be easier to convey the sincerity of your gratitude.

5.  Reduce the number of newsletters to which you subscribe. If you keep trashing a newsletter, unsubscribe.

6.  Be ruthless about reducing the amount of spam/junk email. Block it/report it and make sure you empty the Junk folder regularly.

7.  Reduce the number of people to whom you send each email. Be judicious and ask yourself: does everyone in the To/Cc box really need your email? Or are you sending it to so many people for your own self-gratification?

8.  Don't be so quick to send that follow-up chaser email. Recognise that others may not have the same priorities as you. If the matter is urgent, try talking.

9.  Keep your email messages as short as possible but not so short that they become trivial. Cut out all the unnecessary fluff and chatter.

10. Clean out your inbox regularly and at least once every three months to keep the size down. Yes, most of us now have nearly unlimited inbox storage capacity, but remember, the bigger the inbox, the more $CO_2$ is needed to preserve it in working order. If you only do this occasionally, then why not join 'Clean Inbox Week' – always the third week of January.

In summary, 'small' creates a beautiful carbon footprint when it comes to email and inbox size. At the same time, make sure you don't send trivial one-line message which have no value for the recipient (for example, 'OK', 'Thanks', 'Will do'). Chrome has a neat extension called 'Carbon Caper' which pops up when you send an email of less than four words to prompt you to think whether or not you need to send the email.

Over time, as reducing our carbon footprint becomes increasingly pressing, you can expect more extensions and apps like this one to help make your individual effort feel less like a drop in the ocean and more like a significant contribution to addressing climate change. Lastly, addressing the email carbon footprint is another area where you stand out as a beacon of success.

# ...AND ALL THE REST!

# Tip #95

## External Survey Applications

## The Challenge

Getting feedback from people external to your organisation can be somewhat of a challenge. In these chapters, we uncover three ways to get feedback.

- Getting Feedback: Outlook Voting Buttons
- Getting Feedback: Google Forms
- Getting Feedback: Microsoft Forms

However, each has their limitations. For example, Outlook voting buttons really work best if everyone is using Outlook and even better if they're all on the same Exchange server. Google and Microsoft Forms apps are extremely easy to use and deliver data in a format which you can use. However, some organisations may be blocking these apps for security reasons.

If you need a robust alternative that gets past these limitations, you may need to look outside of your primary office productivity suite to an online survey tool.

## The Solution

PC Magazine (pcmag.com) rated online survey apps for 2020 (https://www.pcmag.com/picks/the-best-online-survey-tools) and came up with these as their top 10 (June 8, 2019).

Some well-known names popped up as well as a few newcomers. Some are free, others, free to try. Most will charge you something and the price range is wide. Here are their top 10.

1. Qualtrics – qualtrics.com
2. Zoho Survey – zoho.com/survey
3. Alchemer (formerly Survey Gizmo) – alchemer.com
4. SoGoSurvey – sogosurvey.com
5. SurveyMonkey – surveymonkey.com
6. WorldApp KeySurvey – keysurvey.com
7. Checkbox Survey – checkbox.com
8. Survey Planet – surveyplanet.com
9. Outside Software eSurveysPro – esurveyspro.com
10. Toluna QuickSurveys – quicksurveys.com

## How to Choose

When one is reviewing apps for a particular purpose, you will find similarities amongst the pros and cons. However, an evaluation of these types of tools yields a wide variety of features and drawbacks. Before diving in, be sure you know the following.

- **Technical skills of the survey creators** – Some of these tools are rated highly because the user interface is easy and straightforward. If you need a robust option that is also complicated to use, factor in training to the entire cost of acquisition. Also check out how robust the user help resources are, both within the product and in online training portals.

- **Types of questions you will need to ask** (multiple choice, branching, multimedia responses) – Not all products offer all types of questions.

- **What do you want to do your analysis in (for example, Excel or Sheets)?** – Some products only provide the analysis tools within the app. Others provide exports or integration to the tools you want to use.

- **Budget** – This should not be the sole factor in your decision. The least expensive options sometimes have the most limitations as to the types of questions or integrations you may have access to.

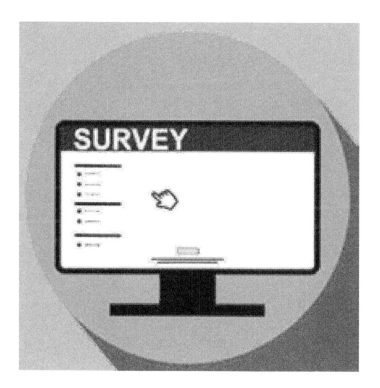

# | Tip #96 |

## Getting Feedback: Google Forms

## The Challenge

Asking several questions to multiple people in an email message might cost you unnecessary hours of processing answers. As discussed in 'Getting Feedback: Microsoft Forms' and 'Getting Feedback: Outlook Voting Buttons', some may put their responses in line with your questions. Others may write a long narrative explaining each choice they've made. Some may separate their answers completely from the questions.

## The Solution

One way to get the answers you need in a format you can use is to use Google Forms. Creating Google Forms is easy and there are multiple options for the types of questions you can ask and the content respondents can use in their answers. This solution assumes you've set up a Gmail account. It does not matter whether this is from the free version or Google Workspace. By default, feedback comes to you anonymously. You may create questions to request an email address. Please be sure your organisation can remain compliant with regulations regarding collection of contact information before adding the question.

## Creating the Form

1.  In your browser, in the URL field, type: forms.google.com. Click the + Blank tile or choose from one of the templates. You can also begin a form from Google Drive. Click the New button and choose Google Forms from the drop-down list.

2.  Title your form and choose the question type you wish to use.

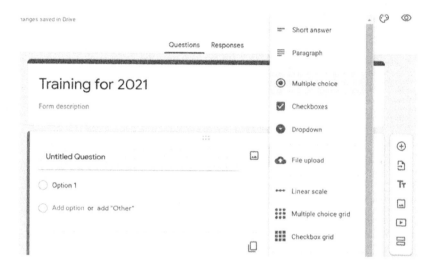

3.  As you type your question, Google will try to guess the type of responses you may want. For example, if it detects a yes or no question, it may offer to put this in with a one-click operation.

4.  Click the Preview button at the top right (looks like an eye) to see what your form will look like to your recipients.

5.  When you're done adding questions and previewing the form, click the Send button in the upper right corner.

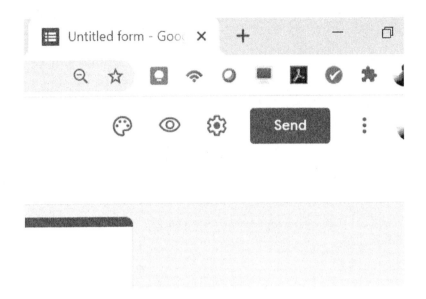

6. You can choose to email the form, create a link or get the embed code for an html page.

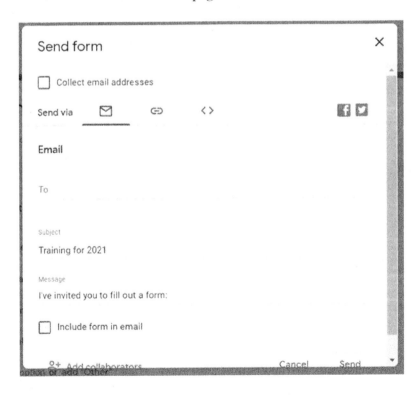

> **Pro Tip:**
>
> To send to a large number of recipients, it might be easier to use a mail merge. Capture the link on the above dialogue by clicking the link symbol (middle symbol to the right of 'Send via') and paste it in your merge document. (See 'Performing a Mail Merge from Outlook' and 'Mail Merge in Gmail'.)

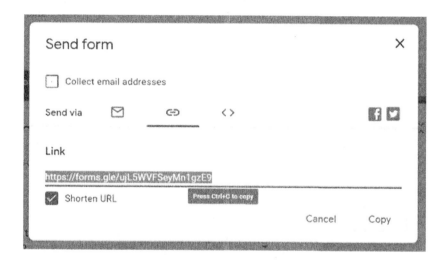

## More Options

By clicking the = sign in the tool-bar to the right of your form, you can create sections. This will allow you to establish branching logic. Branching logic will direct respondents to a different set of questions depending upon their response to a previous one. For example, if respondents indicated that they took Office Technology training in 2020, you could direct them to a list of topics for them to choose the courses they took.

1. First add all the sections you will need to complete your form.

2. Then, back on the question that will direct them to the appropriate question, click the vertical ellipses in the lower right corner of the question area and choose 'Go to section based on answer'.

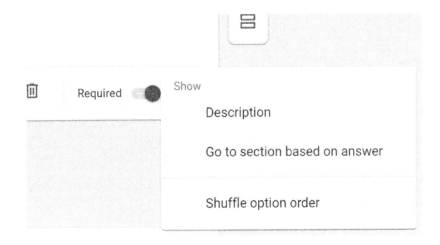

3. In the case of a multiple-choice question like ours, drop-down buttons will appear allowing you to determine where the respondent will go next based on their answer.

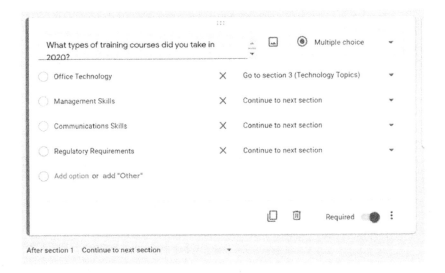

## Processing Responses

To find responses, locate your form either in the folder in which you created it or by returning to forms.google.com. You should see it listed there.

As responses come in, you may view them individually, as a summary or in Google Sheets. To see all the data in a spreadsheet, click the Google Sheets icon at the top right.

# ‖ Tip #97 ‖

## Getting Feedback: Microsoft Forms

## The Challenge

A wise person once said, 'Don't ask an engineer what time it is. They'll tell you how to build a watch.' If you're trying to get feedback from your colleagues, asking them questions in email might yield all sorts of data. Now you've added time to the back end of this task by needing to sift through what you've been given just to learn what you needed to know.

## The Solution

One way to get the answers you need is to use Microsoft Forms. If you've ever used Google Forms, the process is very similar and every bit as easy. There are multiple options for the types of questions you can ask and how respondents can answer. This solution assumes you have any type of Microsoft account. By default, feedback comes to you anonymously. You may opt to request email addresses, but be sure your organisation is compliant with regulations regarding collection of contact information before enabling this option.

## Creating the Form

1. In your browser, in the URL field, type: forms.microsoft.com. Click the New Form or New Quiz tile. You can also begin a form from OneDrive. Click the New button and choose Forms for Excel from the drop-down list.

2. Title your form. Add a description if you wish.

3. Click 'Add new' to start adding questions. You will be offered several different types of questions to add. Click the drop-down arrow for more question types.

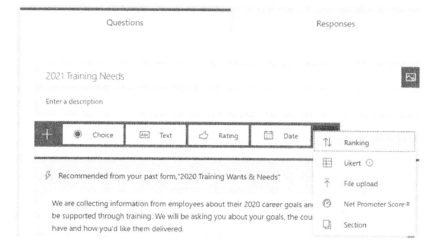

4. As you type your question, Microsoft will try to guess the type of responses you may want. For example, if it detects a yes or no question, it may offer to put this in with a one-click operation.

5. Click the Preview button at the top right to see what your form will look like to your recipients.

6. When you're done adding questions and previewing the form, click the Share button in the upper right corner.

7. You can choose to create a link or a QR code, get the embed code for an html page or email the form.

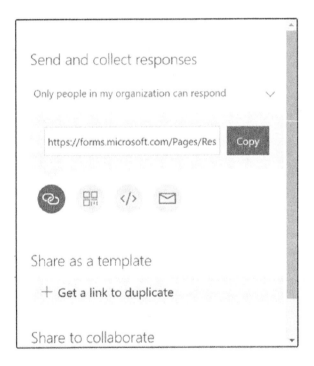

---

**Pro Tip:**

To send to a large number of recipients, it might be easier to use a mail merge. Capture the link on the above dialogue by clicking the link symbol (middle symbol to the right of 'Send via') and paste it in your merge document. (See 'Performing a Mail Merge from Outlook' and 'Mail Merge in Gmail'.)

## More Options

By clicking the ellipses sign at the bottom of a question, you can establish branching logic. Branching logic will direct respondents to a question depending upon their response to a previous one. It is best to enter all of your questions and then add branching logic.

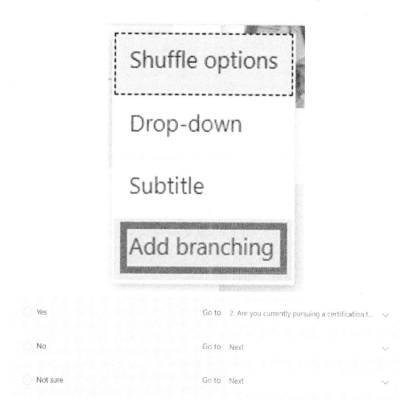

## Processing Responses

To find responses, locate your form either in the folder in which you created it or by returning to forms.microsoft.com. You should see it listed there. As responses come in, you may view them individually, as a summary or in Excel. To see all the data in an Excel workbook, click the Open in Excel link at the top right.

| | A | B | C | D | E | F |
|---|---|---|---|---|---|---|
| 1 | ID | Start time | Completion time | Email | Name | We are collecting inf |
| 2 | 1 | 11/22/20 17:42:23 | 11/22/20 17:43:13 | melissa@memct.com | Melissa Esquibel | Yes |
| 3 | 2 | 11/22/20 17:43:18 | 11/22/20 17:43:48 | melissa@memct.com | Melissa Esquibel | No |

## What About Google Forms?

Generally speaking, you would choose the Forms app that is within your productivity platform ecosystem (for example, Google Forms for Google Workspace platforms and Microsoft Forms for Microsoft platforms). They are both equally easy to use and very similar in features. (See 'Getting Feedback: Google Forms').

# Tip #98

## Group Soup in Outlook

### The Challenge

Groups mean two different things in the Microsoft universe. Do you know which one to use? Let's clear it up.

New Contact    New Group    New Contact Group    New Items ⌄

New

### The Solution

Remember something called a distribution list? That's an email list that you can use to send the same message to a group of people. In Outlook, this is known as a Contact Group. To create one:

1. From the People window, click the New Contact Group button.
2. Click the Add Members button on the next screen.
3. Choose how you wish to add members.

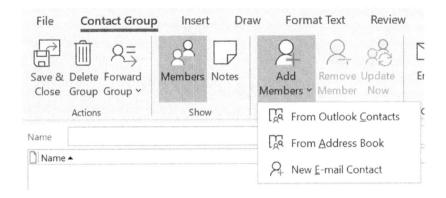

4. If you choose New E-mail Contact, the member will be added to your distribution list and cause a new contact to be added to your My Contacts.

A Group is another entity altogether, though it can be used to communicate with multiple people. When you click New Group in the ribbon, here is what you are creating.

- Active Directory group
- SharePoint site
- Document library
- A hub to connect other services like Trello, Azure, Yammer and Mail-Chimp

The ability to do all this will be contained in a message that appears when you click on the Group you created in Groups in the Mail window.

# The new Website Rework Project group is ready

 **Website Rework Project**
To Website Rework Project

ⓘ If there are problems with how this message is displayed, click here to view it in a web browser.

### Start a conversation

Read group conversations or start your own.

### Add to the team site

Start sharing and collaborating on content in SharePoint.

### Share files

View, edit, and share all group files, including email attachments.

### Connect your apps

Connect apps like Twitter and Trello to stay current with information and updates your team cares about.

1. And, there's more! You can add this group to the Teams app and get even more collaboration tools. From Teams, click on 'Join or create a team' in the lower left corner of the Teams window.

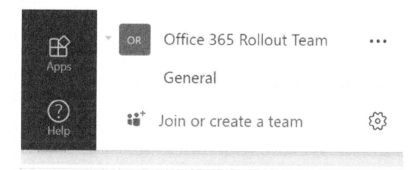

2. Click the Create Team button on the next screen.

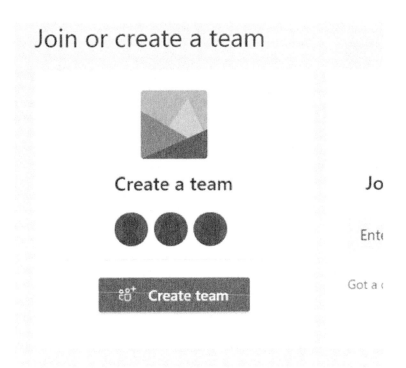

3. On the next screen, you can click 'From a group or team'.

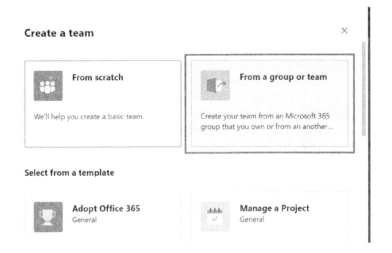

4. On the next screen, choose Microsoft 365 group.

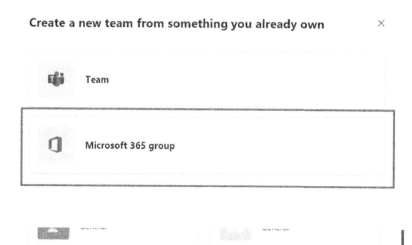

5. Choose your group from the next dialogue.

# | Tip #99 |

## Use Smart Lookup in Microsoft Office

## The Challenge

When creating documents, spreadsheets and presentations, especially on new topics, it can be challenging to be flipping to new screens to research images, content and definitions. Just like the pre-internet days, it is always easiest to work surrounded by the reference books you need while you were working.

## The Solution

Enter Smart Lookup. This feature is enabled out of the box in Word, Excel, Outlook and PowerPoint. You can stay in the application and search for what you need. Smart Lookup will deliver the information in a task pane on the right side of the application window. The feature is available on the PC and in Office for Mac.

## How It Works

1. At the top right of the ribbon, you will see the Search field. It is in the same location on each of the applications. You can also access this with Alt+Q on a PC. If you are using it in Outlook, be sure you are composing an item, such as an email, first.

2. Type the keywords of the material you need (for example, 'fractal geometry.'

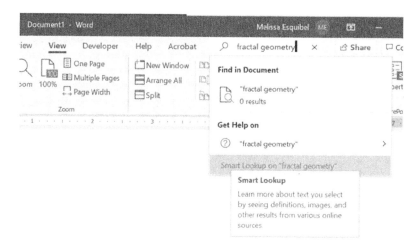

3. In the drop-down list from the Search field, you'll see 'Smart Lookup on [your search terms]'. Click that to reveal the panel on the right.

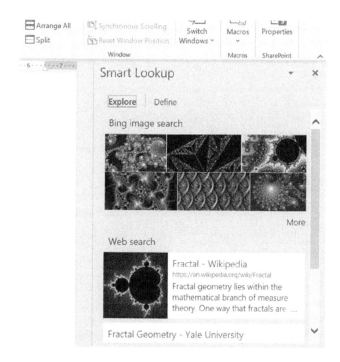

## Using Smart Lookup Results

If you're looking for images, you can simply right-click the desired image from the search results and copy, then paste it into your document. If you want to see more images, click the More link. If you want to know more about the images themselves, just click on an image to be taken to the search results page in your default browser.

To access content, click on the thumbnails of web search results to be taken to the page with the full information. This section also has a More button to find more search results. The best news is after you are done reviewing what you've found, when you close the windows and return to Word, the task pane is still there! This helps you avoid having too many windows open and losing important bits of information.

# ‖ Tip #100 ‖

## Are You a Technology Leader or Follower?

*Imagination is more important than knowledge. For knowledge is limited, whereas imagination embraces the entire world, stimulating progress, giving birth to evolution.*
*— Albert Einstein*

## The Challenge

There is now no doubt that top PAs and EAs are expected to be proficient with all their productivity tools, like Microsoft Office and G Suite. Indeed, most surveys rate such skills within the top three that they demand from any high-flying PA or EA. Given that these are probably now the basic tools of the trade, the challenge is, how do you differentiate your technological expertise? Does this mean you always have to be working at the bleeding edge of any technological development (a leader often called an early adopter), or can you be a follower (late adopter)?.

## The Solution

When Bette Nesmith Graham invented Liquid Paper, the power of innovation among those in the administrative professions could no longer be dismissed.

Most of us are more likely to harness the power of the technology provided to us and develop smarter ways of working, especially as new ways of office work emerge.

You help yourself stand out from the crowds by owning your power to innovate. There are attitudes and personality traits that can be cultivated to become an innovation leader.

## Attitude and Personality Traits Towards Technology

Develop the following attitudes and personality traits towards technology:

- Imagination. When you are doing a task, always imagine how technology could help you do it better. You can be sure there is probably an app out there which you can try. A perfect example of this is an EA who decided to trial OneNote, a notetaking app developed by Microsoft, with her executive as a way of collecting together all the papers her executive needed each day, from reports to travel papers. Previously, she would laboriously assemble these into a conventional paper-based folder. Now, they all go in their OneNote 'Digital Notebook'. In her words, this has 'helped us to maximise the productivity of the CEO's office, optimising our working day and allowing us to work smarter and faster'.

- Love technology. You may not be a digital native, but that should not stop you. If necessary, find a tech-savvy person to mentor you in exchange for you mentoring them about those aspects of being a good PA/EA in which you are strongest, such as discretion, maintaining confidentiality and influencing work processes.

- Learn one new function each week of the specific everyday tools you use and share it with colleagues. See 'Create a Desk Manual With OneNote' for ideas on how to collect and share these.

- Keep up to date with technological developments within your own business and the PA/EA world. Subscribe to appropriate technology-related newsletters and social media feeds. See the Pocket app for saving internet articles you don't have time to read, which will automatically curate material for you on specific topics. Good news sources include PC Magazine, Wired, TechRepublic, The Guardian, Fast Company Compass and StackExchange.

- Follow technology leaders on social media and get involved in the conversation.

- Be curious. Create Google Alerts for topics of interest.

- Volunteer to be involved in IT pilot projects related to the tools you will asked to use. Offer your unique perspective on how your colleagues use technology as they interact with you.

- Establish yourself as the go-to person for help on producing documents, spreadsheets and presentations as well as other relevant systems used within your part of the business.

- Many PA/EA networks have technology updates; this is always a good place to pick up ideas. If they don't have one, start one for them.

- Don't be afraid to trial new apps/software. Though you may be limited in your ability to install things on organisation equipment, if you can build a case for looking at something new, IT may very well go along. Don't forget that IT is a service to the business driven by the organisation's needs and not the reverse. Though IT wields a significant sword in its endeavour to keep systems up, running and secure, don't let it keep you from introducing a chance of improving productivity and performance.

- Conversely, recognise when to let go. Nearly all big IT projects which fail do so because the originator will not let go of their original idea. Project sponsors who keep pushing a project forward in the original direction, even though it fails to address changes and new discoveries, detract from an organisation's ability to innovate, to survive and to thrive.

- Consider taking a technology-related qualification – anything from Microsoft Office Specialist or Google Workspace certification to an undergraduate or graduate degree in business or technology.

## To Be a Leader or Follower?

Which you are at any point in time will often depend on your business and your executive. In some instances, you will be in a culture which always adopts the latest technology. Alternatively, you may be in a business which is less technology-focused or perhaps have a boss who is not very tech-savvy. In such cases, try to make sure you are amongst the early adopters of any new implementations, and, be there to support and coach the less technically savvy boss. Leading doesn't always carry a title or a job description. It is not so much about being a leader or follower as it is being a technology champion and making sure you are not left behind when technology emerges which can help you be more productive, effective and efficient.

# ‖ Tip #101 ‖

## Keeping Up With the Changes

## The Challenge

It may seem strange to say that this is *only* 101 Tips. In fact, whittling it down to 101 was a challenge! And we acknowledge that, while you may have found useful tools and suggestions in the collection, it may not have addressed the thing you were most hoping to find here! For better or worse, this is the journey all of us take who utilise technology to get our jobs done. A frequent question we hear is, "How do I keep up with all of what's new and changed?" For those of us in the training profession, it's a daily task that requires patience, diligence, and acceptance that whatever I thought a thing was, it is now different and will be again in a couple of weeks.

## The Solution

# Become a Lifelong Learner

If you have this book, we are probably preaching to the choir. That said, the commitment to continuous learning and acceptance of change is key to whatever strategy you adopt to keep up. In support of your dedication to this commitment, here are a few suggestions to meeting the challenge.

1. *Create a learning diary.* As you go through your day, be aware when you say to yourself:

   - I wonder what that means.
   - I wish I knew more about this.
   - There must be a better way.
   - That's kind of cool! I wonder how that works.

   Take a few seconds to jot down the application or technology this concerns, what happened to make you wonder and just enough details so you can follow-up on it later. Star it if it really sparks your interest (see #3 below). When you find your answers, copy/paste the link where you found it, or the title of the book you used as a resource (see #4 below).

2. *Schedule time each week to consult your learning diary.* Spend even 10 minutes a week looking something up, watching a video or researching resources that will help answer your question. All caught up with your questions, use the time to dig deeper into the places where you found your answers.

3. *Create a glossary from minutes.* If you take minutes in meetings, flag or star items like acronyms or industry-specific terms you don't understand. If you use a repository like OneNote to capture minutes, create a page or section called Glossary. As you go back through your notes, copy the unknown terms and acronyms to this page and look them up. Not only will you gain a better understanding of the proceedings, but you will also gain unique insight into how your organisation utilises technology to meet its objectives.

4. *Share what you learned with a colleague.* The best way to reinforce what you've learned is to immediately share it with someone else. Don't be afraid to let your executive know if you've found something that might improve their work lives. Not only may it have that desired effect, he or she will realise the value of having someone like you on the team.

5. *Pursue that which sparks your interest.* Melissa, for example, is a Microsoft geek. Anytime a new tweet or LinkedIn post addresses a new feature of Excel, she's off after it to see how it works and what it does. She pursues certifications in Microsoft applications and learns even more. What lights up your curiosity? Is there a certification or educational program for it? If you find that there is, go for it! Set a time goal for yourself, whether that's a few months, a year or even two-years for something like an advanced degree. Then make sure you update your CV, resume and/or LinkedIn profile and strut your stuff!

## As you change your productivity will increase

And, as you change your behaviour and acquire new skills sets, your productivity too will increase, as shown below.

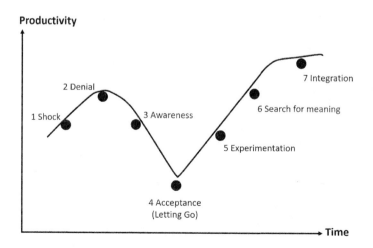

There are seven clearly defined stages to achieving permanent improved productivity no matter what the change (from divorce to changing how and where you work). Most are self-explanatory.

1. Shock – this gives one a perceived temporary boost.

2. Denial – forget it, this will not effect/happen to me. Now you ae in a state of euphoria and feel even more productive.

3. Awareness - you realise that yes, you do need to acquire new skills and behaviours. This generates some doubts about how competent you are and can cope with the new ways and hence rapidly leads to stage 4.

4. Acceptance – the lowest point as you start to realise that change will happen whether you like it or not and without adapting you will be left behind. How long you stay at the low point depends on how quickly you let go of your old habits/behaviors, accept the new norm and acquire the necessary skills to change.

5. Experimentation - learning new skills and behaviors may take time and you need to experiment with what is best for you and your personal situation.

6. Searching for meaning - internalise the new skills/behaviour and what it means for you and your career.

7. Integration – choose which skills/behaviors you will adopt and make them an integral part of your new *modus operandi* (way of working). Then you start to be even more productive as you adapt to the new ways of working be it a new piece of technology, how often you go to the office etc.

Often, we pass through the seven stages almost without realising it. However, sometimes we get stuck and that is when the world passes us by which is why life-long learning is so important.

The key to gaining the maximum benefit from any change is first to work through each stage. Make sure you take time to work through each stage properly (be it minutes to days). Then your productivity gains will be permanent and help you improve your career.

# AUTHORS

## Dr. Monica Seeley

Leading Email Productivity and Etiquette Expert

Dr. Monica Seeley, founder of Mesmo Consultancy, is an international authority on the most effective ways to use email and other digital communications to enhance both personal and business performance. She works all over the world helping individuals and organisations apply best practice to improve their communications and well-being.

Her fifth book, '100 Top Tips to use Digital Communications to Boost Your Performance' summarises in 'easy to read nuggets' how to manage digital communications, especially email, more effectively. Her other books include 'The Executive Secretary Guide to Taking Control of Your Inbox' and 'Brilliant Email'.

Through her one-to-one coaching, workshops and strategic consultancy, those who work with her are able to save time and dramatically reduce information overload, of which email overload has become one of the major drains on people's productivity. Her clients are drawn from a wide range of organisations of all sizes from the public, private and not-for-profit sectors.

Over the past 30 years, she has coached and trained thousands of business executives from CEOs, finance directors, sales, marketing and engineering personnel to executive assistants, personal assistants and receptionists.

Monica has been a Visiting Fellow at Sir John Cass Business School, City University and Bournemouth University Business School. Her research includes the future of email, managing email addiction, alleviating the stress caused by email overload and reducing the level of carbon emissions caused by digital devices.

# Melissa Esquibel, MCT, MOSM

Technology Evangelist,
Educator and Mentor

Melissa Esquibel is a noted speaker in the administrative professional conference. She has presented to hundreds of admin pros all over the world. She is also the 'head chick in charge' of Sawbuck Seminars and purveyor of Watch and Learn, an ever-growing library of online instructional content on office automation. Her passion is to facilitate friendship between people and their technology. She is passionate about administrative professionals finding their seat at the table when it comes to technology decision-making

In addition to this book, in 2019 she released her first book, 'Dirty Data: Excel techniques to turn what you get into what you need'. Though she claims Excel as her 'happy place' she is an expert at all things Microsoft when it comes to office productivity applications. She's also a bit of a Google Workspace nerd as well! She is the editor of ExecSecTech Digest and guest contributor to Administrative Professional Today. She was the principal contributing editor for Office Technology Today. (Administrative Professional Today and Office Technology Today are publications of Capitol Information Group and Business Management Daily).

Born in Chicago, IL, US, she lives with a foot in Chicago and another in Javea, Alicante, Spain. She started in tech, as she says, 'shortly after the earth cooled and the dinosaurs left.' Her technology career progressed from banking and internal controls to data security, disaster recovery and business risk analysis. The skill set was unique in the early '80s, so it allowed her to explore positions in insurance, manufacturing, telecommunications, energy and healthcare.

# INDEX